Contents

The Science of Being Great
Page 5

The Science of Being Well
Page 61

How to Get What You Want: The Science of Being Successful
Page 117

THE SCIENCE OF SUCCESS
THREE BOOKS IN ONE VOLUME

THE SCIENCE OF BEING GREAT

THE SCIENCE OF BEING WELL

HOW TO GET WHAT YOU WANT: THE SCIENCE OF BEING SUCCESSFUL

by
Wallace D. Wattles

Edited by
Jeffrey L. King

CSJ King Publishing
Oregon, Wisconsin
Copyright © 2018 CSJ King Publishing
All rights reserved.

All rights reserved. No part of this book may be reproduced, stored in a retrieval system, or transmitted in any form or by any means, electronic, mechanical, photocopying, recording, or otherwise, without the express written permission of the publisher, except by a reviewer who may quote brief passages in a review to be printed in a newspaper, magazine, or journal.

ISBN-13: 978-0-9856220-8-4
ISBN-10: 0-9856220-8-3

The Science of Being Great

by Wallace D. Wattles

edited by Jeffrey L. King

TABLE OF CONTENTS

Chapter 1, Any Person May Become Great 7
Chapter 2, Heredity and Opportunity 10
Chapter 3, The Source of Power 12
Chapter 4, The Mind of God 14
Chapter 5, Preparation 16
Chapter 6, The Social Point of View 18
Chapter 7, The Individual Point of View 21
Chapter 8, Consecration. 23
Chapter 9, Identification. 25
Chapter 10, Idealization 27
Chapter 11, Realization 29
Chapter 12, Hurry and Habit. 31
Chapter 13, Thought. 33
Chapter 14, Action At Home. 35
Chapter 15, Action Abroad 37
Chapter 16, Some Further Explanations 40
Chapter 17, More About Thought. 42
Chapter 18, Jesus' Idea of Greatness 45
Chapter 19, A View of Evolution. 47
Chapter 20, Serving GOD 49
Chapter 21, A Mental Exercise 52
Chapter 22, A Summary of the Science of Being Great. 55

Chapter 1
Any Person May Become Great

THERE is a Principle of Power in every person. By the intelligent use and direction of this principle, man can develop his own mental faculties. Man has an inherent power by which he may grow in whatsoever direction he pleases, and there does not appear to be any limit to the possibilities of his growth. No man has yet become so great in any faculty but that it is possible for someone else to become greater. The possibility is in the Original Substance from which man is made. Genius is Omniscience flowing into man.

Genius is more than talent. Talent may merely be one faculty developed out of proportion to other faculties, but genius is the union of man and God in the acts of the soul. Great men are always greater than their deeds. They are in connection with a reserve of power that is without limit. We do not know where the boundary of the mental powers of man is; we do not even know that there is a boundary.

The power of conscious growth is not given to the lower animals; it is man's alone and may be developed and increased by him. The lower animals can, to a great extent, be trained and developed by man; but man can train and develop himself. He alone has this power, and he has it to an apparently unlimited extent.

The purpose of life for man is growth, just as the purpose of life for trees and plants is growth. Trees and plants grow automatically and along fixed lines; man can grow, as he will. Trees and plants can only develop certain possibilities and characteristics; man can develop any power, which is or has been shown by any person, anywhere. Nothing that is possible in spirit is impossible in flesh and blood. Nothing that man can think is impossible-in action. Nothing that man can imagine is impossible of realization.

Man is formed for growth, and he is under the necessity of growing.

It is essential to his happiness that he should continuously advance. Life without progress becomes unendurable, and the person who ceases from growth must either become imbecile or insane. The greater and more harmonious and well rounded his growth, the happier man will be.

There is no possibility in any man that is not in every man; but if they proceed naturally, no two men will grow into the same thing, or be alike. Every man comes into the world with a predisposition to grow along certain lines, and growth is easier for him along those lines than in any other way. This is a wise provision, for it gives endless variety. It is as if a gardener should throw all his bulbs into one basket; to the superficial observer they would look alike, but growth reveals a tremendous difference. So of men and women, they are like a basket of bulbs. One may be a rose and add brightness and color to some dark corner of the world; one may be a lily and teach a lesson of love and purity to every eye that sees; one may be a climbing vine and hide the rugged outlines of some dark rock; one may be a great oak among whose boughs the birds shall nest and sing, and beneath whose shade the flocks shall rest at noon, but every one will be something worthwhile, something rare, something perfect.

There are undreamed of possibilities in the common lives all around us in a large sense, there are no "common" people. In times of national stress and peril the cracker-box loafer of the corner store and the village drunkard become heroes and statesmen through the quickening of the Principle of Power within them. There is a genius in every man and woman, waiting to be brought forth. Every village has its great man or woman; someone to whom all go for advice in time of trouble; someone who is instinctively recognized as being great in wisdom and insight. To such a one the minds of the whole community turn in times of local crisis; he is tacitly recognized as being great. He does small things in a great way. He could do great things as well if he did but undertake them; so can any man; so can you. The Principle of Power gives us just what we ask of it; if we only undertake little things, it only gives us power for little things; but if we try to do great things in a great way it gives us all the power there is.

But beware of undertaking great things in a small way: of that we shall speak farther on.

There are two mental attitudes a man may take. One makes him like a football. It has resilience and reacts strongly when force is applied to it, but it originates nothing; it never acts of itself. There is no power within it. Men of this type are controlled by circumstances and environment, their destinies are decided by things external to themselves. The Principle of Power within them is never really active at all. They never speak or act from within. The other attitude makes man like a flowing spring. Power comes out from the center of him. He has within him a well of water springing up into everlasting life, he radiates force; he is felt by his environment. The Principle of Power in him is in constant action. He is self-active. "He hath life in himself."

No greater good can come to any man or woman than to become self-active. All the experiences of life are designed by Providence to force men and women into self activity; to compel them to cease being creatures of circumstances and master their environment. In his lowest stage, man is the child of chance and circumstance and the slave of fear. His acts are all reactions resulting from the impingement upon him of forces in his environment. He acts only as he is acted upon; he originates nothing. But the lowest savage has within him a Principle of Power sufficient to master all that he fears; and if he learns this and becomes self-active, he becomes as one of the gods.

The awakening of the Principle of Power in man is the real conversion; the passing from death to life. It is when the dead hear the voice of the Son of Man and come forth and live. It is the resurrection and the life. When it is awakened, man becomes a son of the Highest and all power is given to him in heaven and on earth.

Nothing was ever in any man that is not in you; no man ever had more spiritual or mental power than you can attain, or did greater things than you can accomplish. You can become what you want to be.

Chapter 2
Heredity and Opportunity

YOU are not barred from attaining greatness by heredity. No matter who or what your ancestors may have been or how unlearned or lowly their station, the upward way is open for you. There is no such thing as inheriting a fixed mental position; no matter how small the mental capital we receive from our parents, it may be increased; no man is born incapable of growth.

Heredity counts for something. We are born with subconscious mental tendencies; as, for instance, a tendency to melancholy, or cowardice, or to ill temper; but all these subconscious tendencies may be overcome. When the real man awakens and comes forth he can throw them off very easily. Nothing of this kind need keep you down; if you have inherited undesirable mental tendencies, you can eliminate them and put desirable tendencies in their places. An inherited mental trait is a habit of thought of your father or mother impressed upon your subconscious mind; you can substitute the opposite impression by forming the opposite habit of thought. You can substitute a habit of cheerfulness for a tendency to despondency; you can overcome cowardice or ill temper.

Heredity may count for something, too, in an inherited conformation of the skull. There is something in phrenology, if not as much as its exponents claim; it is true that the different faculties are localized in the brain, and that the power of a faculty depends upon the number of active brain cells in its area. A faculty whose brain area is large is likely to act with more power than one whose cranial section is small; hence persons with certain conformations of the skull show talent as musicians, orators, mechanics, and so on. It has been argued from this that a man's cranial formation must, to a great extent, decide his station in life, but this is an error. It has been found that a small brain section, with many fine and active cells, gives as powerful expression to faculty as a larger brain with coarser cells; and it has been found that by turning the Principle of Power into any section of the brain, with the will and purpose to develop a particular talent, the brain cells may be multiplied indefinitely. Any faculty, power, or talent you possess, no matter how small or rudimentary, may be increased; you can multiply the brain cells in this particular area until it acts as powerfully as you wish. It is true that you can act most easily through those faculties that are now most largely developed; you can do, with the least effort, the things which "come naturally"; but it is also true that if you will make the necessary effort you can develop any talent. You can do what you desire to do and become what you want to be. When you fix upon some ideal and proceed

The Science of Being Great

as hereinafter directed, all the power of your being is turned into the faculties required in the realization of that ideal; more blood and nerve force go to the corresponding sections of the brain, and the cells are quickened, increased, and multiplied in number. The proper use of the mind of man will build a brain capable of doing what the mind wants to do.

The brain does not make the man; the man makes the brain.

Your place in life is not fixed by heredity.

Nor are you condemned to the lower levels by circumstances or lack of opportunity. The Principle of Power in man is sufficient for all the requirements of his soul. No possible combination of circumstances can keep him down, if he makes his personal attitude right and determines to rise. The power, which formed man and purposed him for growth, also controls the circumstances of society, industry, and government; and this power is never divided against itself. The power which is in you is in the things around you, and when you begin to move forward, the things will arrange themselves for your advantage, as described in later chapters of this book. Man was formed for growth, and all things external were designed to promote his growth. No sooner does a man awaken his soul and enter on the advancing way than he finds that not only is God for him, but nature, society, and his fellow men are for him also; and all things work together for his good if he obeys the law. Poverty is no bar to greatness, for poverty can always be removed. Martin Luther, as a child, sang in the streets for bread. Linnaeus the naturalist had only forty dollars with which to educate himself; he mended his own shoes and often had to beg meals from his friends. Hugh Miller, apprenticed to a stonemason, began to study geology in a quarry. George Stephenson, inventor of the locomotive engine, and one of the greatest of civil engineers, was a coal miner, working in a mine, when he awakened and began to think. James Watt was a sickly child, and was not strong enough to be sent to school. Abraham Lincoln was a poor boy. In each of these cases we see a Principle of Power in the man that lifts him above all opposition and adversity.

There is a Principle of Power in you; if you use it and apply it in a certain way you can overcome all heredity, and master all circumstances and conditions and become a great and powerful personality.

Chapter 3
The Source of Power

MAN'S brain, body, mind, faculties, and talents are the mere instruments he uses in demonstrating greatness; in themselves they do not make him great. A man may have a large brain and a good mind, strong faculties, and brilliant talents, and yet he is not a great man unless he uses all these in a great way. That quality which enables man to use his abilities in a great way makes him great; and to that quality we give the name of wisdom. Wisdom is the essential basis of greatness.

Wisdom is the power to perceive the best ends to aim at and the best means for reaching those ends. It is the power to perceive the right thing to do. The man who is wise enough to know the right thing to do, who is good enough to wish to do only the right thing, and who is able and strong enough to do the right thing is a truly great man. He will instantly become marked as a personality of power in any community and men will delight to do him honor.

Wisdom is dependent upon knowledge. Where there is complete ignorance there can be no wisdom, no knowledge of the right thing to do. Man's knowledge is comparatively limited and so his wisdom must be small, unless he can connect his mind with knowledge greater than his own and draw from it, by inspiration, the wisdom that his own limitations deny him. This he can do; this is what the really great men and women have done. Man's knowledge is limited and uncertain; therefore he cannot have wisdom in himself.

Only God knows all truth; therefore only God can have real wisdom or the right thing to do at all times, and man can receive wisdom from God. I proceed to give an illustration: Abraham Lincoln had limited education; but he had the power to perceive truth. In Lincoln we see pre-eminently apparent the fact that real wisdom consists in knowing the right thing to do at all times and under all circumstances; in having the will to do the right thing, and in having talent and ability enough to be competent and able to do the right thing. Back in the days of the abolition agitation, and during the compromise period, when all other men were more or less confused as to what was right or as to what ought to be done, Lincoln was never uncertain. He saw through the superficial arguments of the pro-slavery men; he saw, also, the impracticability and fanaticism of the abolitionists; he saw the right ends to aim at and he saw the best means to attain those ends. It was because men recognized that he perceived truth and knew the right thing to do that they made him president. Any man who develops the power to perceive truth, and who can show that he always knows the right thing to do and that he can be trusted to do the right thing, will be honored and advanced; the whole world is looking eagerly for such men.

When Lincoln became president he was surrounded by a multitude of so-called able advisers, hardly any two of whom were agreed. At times they were all opposed to his policies; at times almost the whole North was opposed to what he proposed to do. But he saw the truth when others were misled by appearances; his judgment was seldom or never wrong. He was at once the ablest statesman and the best soldier of the period. Where did he, a comparatively unlearned man, get this wisdom? It was not due to some peculiar formation of his skull or to some fineness of texture of his brain. It was not due to some physical characteristic. It was not even a quality of mind due to superior reasoning power.

Processes of reason do not often reach knowledge of truth.

It was due to a spiritual insight. He perceived truth, but where did he perceive it and whence did the perception come? We see something similar in Washington, whose faith and courage, due to his perception of truth, held the colonies together during the long and often apparently hopeless struggle of the Revolution. We see something of the same thing in the phenomenal genius of Napoleon, who always knew, in military matters, the best means to adopt. We see that the greatness of Napoleon was in nature rather than in Napoleon, and we discover back of Washington and Lincoln something greater than either Washington or Lincoln. We see the same thing in all great men and women. They perceive truth; but truth cannot be perceived until it exists; and there can be no truth until there is a mind to perceive it. Truth does not exist apart from mind. Washington and Lincoln were in touch and communication with a mind that knew all knowledge and contained all truth. The same is true of all who manifest wisdom. Wisdom is obtained by reading the mind of God.

Chapter 4
The Mind of God

THERE is a Cosmic Intelligence that is in all things and through all things. This is the one real substance. From it all things proceed. It is Intelligent Substance or Mind Stuff. It is God. Where there is no substance there can be no intelligence; for where there is no substance there is nothing. Where there is thought there must be a substance which thinks. Thought cannot be a function; for function is motion, and it is inconceivable that mere motion should think. Thought cannot be vibration, for vibration is motion, and that motion should be intelligent is not thinkable. Motion is nothing but the moving of substance; if there be intelligence shown it must be in the substance and not in the motion. Thought cannot be the result of motions in the brain; if thought is in the brain it must be in the brain's substance and not in the motions which brain substance makes.

But thought is not in the brain substance, for brain substance, without life, is quite unintelligent and dead. Thought is in the life-principle that animates the brain, in the spirit substance, which is the real man. The brain does not think, the man thinks and expresses his thought through the brain.

There is a spirit substance that thinks. Just as the spirit substance of man permeates his body, and thinks and knows in the body, so the Original Spirit Substance, God, permeates all nature and thinks and knows in nature. Nature is as intelligent as man, and knows more than man; nature knows all things. The All-Mind has been in touch with all things from the beginning; and it contains all knowledge. Man's experience covers a few things, and these things man knows; but God's experience covers all the things that have happened since the creation, from the wreck of a planet or the passing of a comet to the fall of a sparrow. All that is and all that has been are present in the Intelligence that is wrapped about us and enfolds us and presses upon us from every side.

All the encyclopedias men have written are but trivial affairs compared to the vast knowledge held by the mind in which men live, move, and have their being.

The truths men perceive by inspiration are thoughts held in this mind. If they were not thoughts men could not perceive them, for they would have no existence; and they could not exist as thoughts unless there is a mind for them to exist in; and a mind can be nothing else than a substance which thinks.

Man is thinking substance, a portion of the Cosmic Substance; but man is limited, while the Cosmic Intelligence from which he sprang, which Jesus calls the Father, is unlimited. All intelligence, power, and force come from the Father. Jesus recognized this and stated it very plainly. Over and over again he ascribed all his wisdom and power to his unity with the Father, and to his perceiving the thoughts of God. "My Father and I are one."

This was the foundation of his knowledge and power. He showed the people the necessity of becoming spiritually awakened; of hearing his voice and becoming like him. He compared the unthinking man who is the prey and sport of circumstances to the dead man in a tomb, and besought him to hear and come forth.

"God is spirit," he said; "be born again, become spiritually awake, and you may see his kingdom. Hear my voice; see what I am and what I do, and come forth and live. The words I speak are spirit and life; accept them and they will cause a well of water to spring up within you. Then you will have life within yourself."

"I do what I see the Father do," he said, meaning that he read the thoughts of God. "The Father shows all things to the son." "If any man has the will to do the will of God, he shall know truth." "My teaching is not my own, but his that sent me." "You shall know the truth and the truth shall make you free." "The spirit shall guide you into all truth."

We are immersed in mind and that mind contains all knowledge and all truth. It is seeking to give us this knowledge, for our Father delights to give good gifts to his children. The prophets and seers and great men and women, past and present, were made great by what they received from God, not by what they were taught by men. This limitless reservoir of wisdom and power is open to you; you can draw upon it, as you will, according to your needs. You can make yourself what you desire to be; you can do what you wish to do; you can have what you want. To accomplish this you must learn to become one with the Father so that you may perceive truth; so that you may have wisdom and know the right ends to seek and the right means to use to attain those ends, and so that you may secure power and ability to use the means. In closing this chapter resolve that you will now lay aside all else and concentrate upon the attainment of conscious unity with God.

"Oh, when I am safe in my sylvan home, I tread on the pride of Greece and Rome, and when I am stretched beneath the pines, where the evening star so holy shines, I laugh at the lore and pride of man, at the Sophist schools and the learned clan, for what are they all in their high conceit, when man in the bush with God may meet?"

Chapter 5
Preparation

"DRAW nigh to God and He will draw nigh to you."

If you become like God you can read his thoughts; and if you do not you will find the inspirational perception of truth impossible.

You can never become a great man or woman until you have overcome anxiety, worry, and fear. It is impossible for an anxious person, a worried one, or a fearful one to perceive truth; all things are distorted and thrown out of their proper relations by such mental states, and those who are in them cannot read the thoughts of God.

If you are poor, or if you are anxious about business or financial matters, you are recommended to study carefully the first volume of this series, "The Science of Getting Rich." That will present to you a solution for your problems of this nature, no matter how large or how complicated they may seem to be. There is not the least cause for worry about financial affairs; every person who wills to do so may rise above want, have all he needs, and become rich. The same source upon which you propose to draw for mental unfolding and spiritual power is at your service for the supply of all your material wants. Study this truth until it is fixed in your thoughts and until anxiety is banished from your mind; enter the Certain Way, which leads to material riches.

Again, if you are anxious or worried about your health, realize it is possible for you to attain perfect health so that you may have strength sufficient for all that you wish to do and more. That Intelligence which stands ready to give you wealth and mental and spiritual power will rejoice to give you health also. Perfect health is yours for the asking, if you will only obey the simple laws of life and live aright. Conquer ill health and cast out fear. But it is not enough to rise above financial and physical anxiety and worry; you must rise above moral evil-doing as well. Sound your inner consciousness now for the motives that actuate you and make sure they are right. You must cast out lust, and cease to be ruled by appetite, and you must begin to govern appetite. You must eat only to satisfy hunger, never for gluttonous pleasure, and in all things you must make the flesh obey the spirit.

You must lay aside greed; have no unworthy motive in your desire to become rich and powerful. It is legitimate and right to desire riches, if you want them for the sake of the soul, but not if you desire them for the lusts of the flesh.

Cast out pride and vanity; have no thought of trying to rule over others or of outdoing them. This is a vital point; there is no temptation so insidious as the selfish desire to rule over others.

Nothing so appeals to the average man or woman as to sit in the uppermost places at feasts, to be respectfully saluted in the market place, and to be called Rabbi, Master. To exercise some sort of control over others is the secret motive of every selfish person. The struggle for power over others is the battle of the competitive world, and you must rise above that world and its motives and aspirations and seek only for life. Cast out envy; you can have all that you want, and you need not envy any man what he has. Above all things see to it that you do not hold malice or enmity toward any one; to do so cuts you off from the mind whose treasures you seek to make your own. "He that loves not his brother, loves not God."

Lay aside all narrow personal ambition and determine to seek the highest good and to be swayed by no unworthy selfishness.

Go over all the foregoing and set these moral temptations out of your heart one by one; determine to keep them out. Then resolve that you will not only abandon all evil thought but that you will forsake all deeds, habits, and courses of action which do not commend themselves to your noblest ideals. This is supremely important; make this resolution with all the power of your soul, and you are ready for the next step toward greatness, which is explained in the following chapter.

Chapter 6
The Social Point of View

"WITHOUT faith it is impossible to please God," and without faith it is impossible for you to become great. The distinguishing characteristic of all really great men and women is an unwavering faith. We see this in Lincoln during the dark days of the war; we see it in Washington at Valley Forge; we see it in Livingstone, the crippled missionary, threading the mazes of the dark continent, his soul aflame with the determination to let in the light upon the accursed slave trade, which his soul abhorred; we see it in Luther, and in Frances Willard, in every man and woman who has attained a place on the muster roll of the great ones of the world. Faith — not a faith in one's self or in one's own powers but faith in principle; in the Something Great which upholds right, and which may be relied upon to give us the victory in due time. Without this faith it is not possible for any one to rise to real greatness. The man who has no faith in principle will always be a small man.

Whether you have this faith or not depends upon your point of view. You must learn to see the world as being produced by evolution, as a something that is evolving and becoming, not as a finished work. Millions of years ago God worked with very low and crude forms of life, low and crude, yet each perfect after its kind. Higher and more complex organisms, animal and vegetable, appeared through the successive ages; the earth passed through stage after stage in its unfolding, each stage perfect in itself, and to be succeeded by a higher one. What I wish you to note is that the so-called "lower organisms" are as perfect after their kind as the higher ones; that the world in the Eocene period was perfect for that period; it was perfect, but God's work was not finished. This is true of the world today. Physically, socially, and industrially it is all good, and it is all perfect. It is not complete anywhere or in any part, but so far as the handiwork of God has gone it is perfect.

THIS MUST BE YOUR POINT OF VIEW: THAT THE WORLD AND ALL IT CONTAINS IS PERFECT, THOUGH NOT COMPLETED.

"All's right with the world." That is the great fact. There is nothing wrong with anything; there is nothing wrong with anybody.

All the facts of life you must contemplate from this standpoint.

There is nothing wrong with nature. Nature is a great advancing presence working beneficently for the happiness of all. All things in Nature are good; she has no evil. She is not completed; for creation is still unfinished, but she is going on to give to man even more bountifully than she has given to him in the past. Nature is a partial expression of God, and God is love. She is perfect but not complete.

So it is of human society and government, although there are trusts and combinations of capital and strikes and lockouts and so on. All these things are part of the forward movement; they are incidental to the evolutionary process of completing society. When it is complete there will be harmony; but it cannot be completed without them. J. P. Morgan is as necessary to the coming social order as the strange animals of the age of reptiles were to the life of the succeeding period, and just as these animals were perfect after their kind, so Morgan is perfect after his kind.

Behold it is all very good. See government and industry as being perfect now, and as advancing rapidly toward being complete; then you will understand that there is nothing to fear, no cause for anxiety, nothing to worry about. Never complain of any of these things. They are perfect; this is the very best possible world for the stage of development man has reached.

This will sound like rank folly to many, perhaps to most people. "What!" they will say, "are not child labor and the exploitation of men and women in filthy and unsanitary factories evil things? Aren't saloons evil? Do you mean to say that we shall accept all these and call them good?"

Child labor and similar things are no more evil than the way of living and the habits and practices of the cave dweller were evil. His ways were those of the savage stage of man's growth, and for that stage they were perfect. Our Industrial practices are those of the savage stage of industrial development, and they are also perfect. Nothing better is possible until we cease to be mental savages in industry and business, and become men and women. This can only come about by the rise of the whole race to a higher viewpoint. And this can only come about by the rise of such individuals here and there as are ready for the higher viewpoint. The cure for all this inharmoniousness lies not with the masters or employers but with the workers themselves. Whenever they reach a higher viewpoint, whenever they shall desire to do so, they can establish complete brotherhood and harmony in Industry; they have the numbers and the power. They are getting now what they desire. Whenever they desire more in the way of a higher, purer, more harmonious life, they will receive more. True, they want more now, but they only want more of the things that make for animal enjoyment, and so industry remains in the savage, brutal, animal stage; when the workers begin to rise to the mental plane of living and ask for more of the things that make for the life of the mind and soul, industry will at once be raised above the plane of savagery and brutality. But it is perfect now upon its plane, behold, in fact it is all very good. So it is true of saloons and dens of vice. If the majority of the people desire these things, it is right and necessary that they should have them. When the majority desires a world without such discords, they will create such a world. So long as men and women are on the plane of bestial thought, so long the social order will be in part disorder, and will show bestial manifestations. The people make society what it is, and as the people rise above the bestial thought, society will rise above the beastly in its manifestations. But a society which thinks in a bestial way must have saloons and dives; it is perfect after its kind, as the world was in the Eocene period, and very good.

All this does not prevent you from working for better things.

You can work to complete an unfinished society, instead of to renovate a decaying one; and you can work with a better heart and a more hopeful spirit. It will make an immense difference with your faith and spirit whether you look upon civilization as a good thing that is becoming better or as a bad and evil thing that is decaying. One viewpoint gives you an advancing and expanding mind and the other gives you a descending and decreasing mind.

One viewpoint will make you grow greater and the other will inevitably cause you to grow smaller. One will enable you to work for the eternal things; to do large works in a great way toward the completing of all that is incomplete and inharmonious; and the other will make you a mere patchwork reformer, working almost without hope to save a few lost souls from what you will grow to consider a lost and doomed world. So you see it makes a vast difference to you, this matter of the social viewpoint. "All's right with the world. Nothing can possibly be wrong but my personal attitude, and I will make that right. I will see the facts of nature and all the events, circumstances, and conditions of society, politics, government, and industry from the highest viewpoint. It is all perfect, though incomplete. It is all the handiwork of God; behold, it is all very good."

Chapter 7
The Individual Point of View

IMPORTANT as the matter of your point of view for the facts of social life is, it is of less moment than your viewpoint for your fellow men, for your acquaintances, friends, relatives, your immediate family, and, most of all, yourself. You must learn not to look upon the world as a lost and decaying thing but as a something perfect and glorious which is going on to a most beautiful completeness; and you must learn to see men and women not as lost and accursed things, but as perfect beings advancing to become complete. There are no "bad" or "evil" people. An engine, which is on the rails pulling a heavy train, is perfect after its kind, and it is good. The power of steam, which drives it, is good. Let a broken rail throw the engine into the ditch, and it does not become bad or evil by being so displaced; it is a perfectly good engine, but off the track. The power of steam that drives it into the ditch and wrecks it is not evil, but a perfectly good power. So that which is misplaced or applied in an incomplete or partial way is not evil. There are no evil people; there are perfectly good people who are off the track, but they do not need condemnation or punishment; they only need to get upon the rails again.

That which is undeveloped or incomplete often appears to us as evil because of the way we have trained ourselves to think. The root of a bulb that shall produce a white lily is an unsightly thing; one might look upon it with disgust. But how foolish we should be to condemn the bulb for its appearance when we know the lily is within it. The root is perfect after its kind; it is a perfect but incomplete lily, and so we must learn to look upon every man and woman, no matter how unlovely in outward manifestation; they are perfect in their stage of being and they are becoming complete. Behold, it is all very good.

Once we come into a comprehension of this fact and arrive at this point of view, we lose all desire to find fault with people, to judge them, criticize them, or condemn them. We no longer work as those who are saving lost souls, but as those who are among the angels, working out the completion of a glorious heaven. We are born of the spirit and we see the kingdom of God. We no longer see men as trees walking, but our vision is complete. We have nothing but good words to say. It is all good; a great and glorious humanity coming to completeness. And in our association with men this puts us into an expansive and enlarging attitude of mind; we see them as great beings and we begin to deal with them and their affairs in a great way. But if we fall to the other point of view and see a lost and degenerate race we shrink into the contracting mind; and our dealings with men and their affairs will be in a small and contracted way. Remember to hold steadily to this point of view; if you do you cannot fail to begin at once to deal with your acquaintances and neighbors and with your own family as a great personality deals with men. This same viewpoint must be the one from which you regard yourself. You must always see yourself as a great advancing soul. Learn to say: "There is THAT in me of which I am made, which knows no imperfection, weakness, or sickness. The world is incomplete, but God in my own consciousness is both perfect and complete. Nothing can be wrong but my own personal attitude, and my own personal attitude can be wrong only when I disobey THAT which is within. I am a perfect manifestation of God so far as I have gone, and I will press on to be complete. I will trust and not be afraid." When you are able to say this understandingly you will have lost all fear and you will be far advanced upon the road to the development of a great and powerful personality.

Chapter 8
Consecration

HAVING attained to the viewpoint that puts you into the right relations with the world and with your fellow men, the next step is consecration; and consecration in its true sense simply means obedience to the soul. You have that within you that which is always impelling you toward the upward and advancing way; and that impelling something is the divine Principle of Power; you must obey it without question. No one will deny the statement that if you are to be great, the greatness must be a manifestation of something within; nor can you question that this something must be the very greatest and highest that is within. It is not the mind, or the intellect, or the reason. You cannot be great if you go no farther back for principle than to your reasoning power. Reason knows neither principle nor morality. Your reason is like a lawyer in that it will argue for either side. The intellect of a thief will plan robbery and murder as readily as the intellect of a saint will plan a great philanthropy. Intellect helps us to see the best means and manner of doing the right thing, but intellect never shows us the right thing. Intellect and reason serve the selfish man for his selfish ends as readily as they serve the unselfish man for his unselfish ends. Use intellect and reason without regard to principle, and you may become known as a very able person, but you will never become known as a person whose life shows the power of real greatness.

There is too much training of the intellect and reasoning powers and too little training in obedience to the soul. This is the only thing that can be wrong with your personal attitude — when it fails to be one of obedience to the Principle of Power.

By going back to your own center you can always find the pure idea of right for every relationship. To be great and to have power it is only necessary to conform your life to the pure idea as you find it in the GREAT WITHIN. Every compromise on this point is made at the expense of a loss of power. This you must remember. There are many ideas in your mind that you have outgrown, and which, from force of habit you still permit to dictate the actions of your life. Cease all this; abandon everything you have outgrown. There are many ignoble customs, social and other, which you still follow, although you know they tend to dwarf and belittle you and keep you acting in a small way. Rise above all this. I do not say that you should absolutely disregard conventionalities, or the commonly accepted standards of right and wrong. You cannot do this; but you can deliver your soul from most of the narrow restrictions that bind the majority of your fellow men. Do not give your time and strength to the support of obsolete institutions, religious or otherwise; do not be bound by creeds in which you do not believe. Be free. You have perhaps formed some sensual habits of mind or body; abandon them. You still indulge in distrustful fears that things will go wrong, or that people will betray you, or mistreat you; get above all of them. You still act selfishly in many ways and on many occasions; cease to do so. Abandon all these, and in place of them put the best actions you can form a conception of in your mind. If you desire to advance, and you are not doing so, remember that it can be only because your thought is better than your practice. You must do as well as you think.

Let your thoughts be ruled by principle, and then live up to your thoughts. Let your attitude in business, in politics, in neighborhood affairs, and in your own home be the expression of the best thoughts you can think. Let your manner toward all men and women, great and small, and especially to your own family circle, always be the most kindly, gracious, and courteous you can picture in your imagination. Remember your viewpoint; you are a god in the company of gods and must conduct yourself accordingly.

The steps to complete consecration are few and simple. You cannot be ruled from below if you are to be great; you must rule from above. Therefore you cannot be governed by physical impulses; you must bring your body into subjection to the mind; but your mind, without principle, may lead you into selfishness and immoral ways. You must put the mind into subjection to the soul, and your soul is limited by the boundaries of your knowledge; you must put it into subjection to that soul which needs no searching of the understanding but before whose eye all things are spread. That constitutes consecration. Say: "I surrender my body to be ruled by my mind; I surrender my mind to be governed by my soul, and I surrender my soul to the guidance of God." Make this consecration complete and thorough, and you have taken the second great step in the way of greatness and power.

Chapter 9
Identification

HAVING recognized God as the advancing presence in nature, society, and your fellow men, and harmonized yourself with all these, and having consecrated yourself to that within you which impels toward the greatest and the highest, the next step is to become aware of and recognize fully the fact that the Principle of Power within you is God Himself. You must consciously identify yourself with the Highest. This is not some false or untrue position to be assumed; it is a fact to be recognized. You are already one with God; you want to become consciously aware of it.

There is one substance, the source of all things, and this substance has within itself the power that creates all things; all power is inherent in it. This substance is conscious and thinks; it works with perfect understanding and intelligence. You know that this is so, because you know that substance exists and that consciousness exists; and that it must be substance that is conscious. Man is conscious and thinks; man is substance, he must be substance, else he is nothing and does not exist at all. If man is substance and thinks, and is conscious, then he is Conscious Substance. It is not conceivable that there should be more than one Conscious Substance; so man is the original substance, the source of all life and power embodied in a physical form. Man cannot be something different from God. Intelligence is one and the same everywhere, and must be everywhere an attribute of the same substance. There cannot be one kind of intelligence in God and another kind of intelligence in man; intelligence can only be in intelligent substance, and Intelligent Substance is God. Man is of one and the same stuff with God, and so all the talents, powers, and possibilities that are in God are in man, not just in a few exceptional men but in everyone. "All power is given to man, in heaven and on earth." "Is it not written, ye are gods?" The Principle of Power in man is man himself, and man himself is God.

But while man is original substance, and has within him all power and possibilities, his consciousness is limited. He does not know all there is to know, and so he is liable to error and mistake. To save himself from these he must unite his mind to that outside him which does know all; he must become consciously one with God. There is a Mind surrounding him on every side, closer than breathing, nearer than hands and feet, and in this mind is the memory of all that has ever happened, from the greatest convulsions of nature in prehistoric days to the fall of a sparrow in this present time; and all that is in existence now as well. Held in this Mind is the great purpose that is behind all nature, and so it knows what is going to be. Man is surrounded by a Mind that knows all there is to know, past, present, and to come.

Everything that men have said or done or written is present there. Man is of the same one identical stuff with this Mind; he proceeded from it; and he can so identify himself with it that he may know what it knows. "My Father is greater than I," said Jesus, "I come from him." "I and my Father are one. He shows the son all things." "The spirit shall guide you into all truth." Your identification of yourself with the Infinite must be accomplished by conscious recognition on your part. Recognizing it as a fact, that there is only God, and that all intelligence is in the one substance, you must affirm this wise statement: "There is only one and that one is everywhere. I surrender myself to conscious unity with the highest. Not I, but the Father. I will to be one with the Supreme and to lead the divine life. I am one with infinite consciousness; there is but one mind, and I am that mind. I that speak unto you am he."

If you have been thorough in the work as outlined in the preceding chapters; if you have attained to the true viewpoint, and if your consecration is complete, you will not find conscious identification hard to attain; and once it is attained, the power you seek is yours, for you have made yourself one with all the power there is.

Chapter 10
Idealization

YOU are a thinking center in original substance, and the thoughts of original substance have creative power; whatever is formed in its thought and held as a thought-form must come into existence as a visible and so-called material form, and a thought-form held in thinking substance is a reality; it is a real thing, whether it has yet become visible to mortal eye or not. This is a fact that you should impress upon your understanding — that a thought held in thinking substance is a real thing; a form, and has actual existence, although it is not visible to you. You internally take the form in which you think of yourself; and you surround yourself with the invisible forms of those things with which you associate in your thoughts.

If you desire a thing, picture it clearly and hold the picture steadily in mind until it becomes a definite thought-form; and if your practices are not such as to separate you from God, the thing you want will come to you in material form. It must do so in obedience to the law by which the universe was created.

Make no thought-form of yourself in connection with disease or sickness, but form a conception of health. Make a thought-form of yourself as strong and hearty and perfectly well; impress this thought-form on creative intelligence, and if your practices are not in violation of the laws by which the physical body is built, your thought-form will become manifest in your flesh. This also is certain; it comes by obedience to law. Make a thought-form of yourself, as you desire to be, and set your ideal as near to perfection as your imagination is capable of forming the conception.

Let me illustrate: If a young law student wishes to become great, let him picture himself (while attending to the viewpoint, consecration, and identification, as previously directed) as a great lawyer, pleading his case with matchless eloquence and power before the judge and jury; as having an unlimited command of truth, of knowledge and of wisdom. Let him picture himself as the great lawyer in every possible situation and contingency; while he is still only the student in all circumstances let him never forget or fail to be the great lawyer in his thought-form of himself. As the thought-form grows more definite and habitual in his mind, the creative energies, both within and without, are set at work, he begins to manifest the form from within and all the essentials without, which go into the picture, begin to be impelled toward him. He makes himself into the image and God works with him; nothing can prevent him from becoming what he wishes to be.

In the same general way the musical student pictures himself as performing perfect harmonies, and as delighting vast audiences; the actor forms the highest conception he is capable of in regard to his art, and applies this conception to himself. The farmer and the mechanic do exactly the same thing. Fix upon your ideal of what you wish to make of yourself; consider well and be sure that you make the right choice; that is, the one that will be the most satisfactory to you in a general way. Do not pay too much attention to the advice or suggestions of those around you: do not believe that anyone can know, better than yourself, what is right for you. Listen to what others have to say, but always form your own conclusions.

DO NOT LET OTHER PEOPLE DECIDE WHAT YOU ARE TO BE. BE WHAT YOU FEEL THAT YOU WANT TO BE.

Do not be misled by a false notion of obligation or duty. You can owe no possible obligation or duty to others that should prevent you from making the most of yourself. Be true to yourself, and you cannot then be false to any man. When you have fully decided what thing you want to be, form the highest conception of that thing that you are capable of imagining, and make that conception a thought-form. Hold that thought-form as a fact, as the real truth about yourself, and believe in it.

Close your ears to all adverse suggestions. Never mind if people call you a fool and a dreamer. Dream on. Remember that Bonaparte, the half-starved lieutenant, always saw himself as the general of armies and the master of France, and he became in outward realization what he held himself to be in mind. So likewise will you. Attend carefully to all that has been said in the preceding chapters, and act as directed in the following ones, and you will become what you want to be.

Chapter 11
Realization

IF you were to stop with the close of the last chapter, however, you would never become great; you would be indeed a mere dreamer of dreams, a castle-builder. Too many do stop there; they do not understand the necessity for present action in realizing the vision and bringing the thought-form into manifestation. Two things are necessary; firstly, the making of the thought-form and secondly, the actual appropriation to yourself of all that goes into, and around, the thought-form. We have discussed the first, now we will proceed to give directions for the second. When you have made your thought-form, you are already, in your interior, what you want to be; next you must become externally what you want to be. You are already great within, but you are not yet doing the great things without. You cannot begin, on the instant, to do the great things; you cannot be before the world the great actor, or lawyer, or musician, or personality you know yourself to be; no one will entrust great things to you as yet for you have not made yourself known. But you can always begin to do small things in a great way.

Here lies the whole secret. You can begin to be great today in your own home, in your store or office, on the street, everywhere; you can begin to make yourself known as great, and you can do this by doing everything you do in a great way. You must put the whole power of your great soul in to every act, however small and commonplace, and so reveal to your family, your friends, and neighbors what you really are. Do not brag or boast of yourself; do not go about telling people what a great personage you are, simply live in a great way. No one will believe you if you tell him you are a great man, but no one can doubt your greatness if you show it in your actions. In your domestic circle be so just, so generous, so courteous, and kindly that your family, your wife, husband, children, brothers, and sisters shall know that you are a great and noble soul. In all your relations with men be great, just, generous, courteous, and kindly. The great are never otherwise. This is your attitude.

Next, and most important, you must have absolute faith in your own perceptions of truth. Never act in haste or hurry; be deliberate in everything; wait until you feel that you know the true way. And when you do feel that you know the true way, be guided by your own faith though the entire world shall disagree with you. If you do not believe what God tells you in little things, you will never draw upon his wisdom and knowledge in larger things. When you feel deeply that a certain act is the right act, do it and have perfect faith that the consequences will be good. When you are deeply impressed that a certain thing is true, no matter what the appearances to the contrary may be, accept that thing as true and act accordingly. The one way to develop a perception of truth in large things is to trust absolutely to your present perception of truth in small things. Remember that you are seeking to develop this very power or faculty — the perception of truth; you are learning to read the thoughts of God. Nothing is great and nothing is small in the sight of Omnipotence; he holds the sun in its place, but he also notes a sparrow's fall, and numbers the hairs of your head.

God is as much interested in the little matters of everyday life as he is in the affairs of nations. You can perceive truth about family and neighborhood affairs as well as about matters of statecraft. And the way to begin is to have perfect faith in the truth in these small matters, as it is revealed to you from day to day. When you feel deeply impelled to take a course that seems contrary to all reason and worldly judgment, take that course. Listen to the suggestions and advice of others, but always do what you feel deeply in the within to be the true thing to do. Rely with absolute faith, at all times, on your own perception of truth; but be sure that you listen to God — that you do not act in haste, fear, or anxiety.

Rely upon your perception of truth in all the facts and circumstances of life. If you deeply feel that a certain man will be in a certain place on a certain day, go there with perfect faith to meet him; he will be there, no matter how unlikely it may seem. If you feel sure that certain people are making certain combinations, or doing certain things, act in the faith that they are doing those things. If you feel sure of the truth of any circumstance or happening, near or distant, past, present, or to come, trust in your perception. You may make occasional mistakes at first because of your imperfect understanding of the within; but you will soon be guided almost invariably right. Soon your family and friends will begin to defer, more and more, to your judgment and to be guided by you. Soon your neighbors and townsmen will be coming to you for counsel and advice; soon you will be recognized as one who is great in small things, and you will be called upon more and more to take charge of larger things. All that is necessary is to be guided absolutely, in all things, by your inner light, your perception of truth. Obey your soul, have perfect faith in yourself. Never think of yourself with doubt or distrust, or as one who makes mistakes. "If I judge, my judgment is just, for I seek not honor from men, but from the Father only."

Chapter 12
Hurry and Habit

NO doubt you have many problems, domestic, social, physical, and financial, which seem to you to be pressing for instant solution.

You have debts that must be paid, or other obligations that must be met; you are unhappily or inharmoniously placed, and feel that something must be done at once. Do not get into a hurry and act from superficial impulses. You can trust God for the solution of all your personal riddles. There is no hurry. There is only God, and all is well with the world.

There is an invincible power in you, and the same power is in the things you want. It is bringing them to you and bringing you to them. This is a thought that you must grasp, and hold continuously that the same intelligence that is in you is in the things you desire. They are impelled toward you as strongly and decidedly as your desire impels you toward them. The tendency, therefore, of a steadily held thought must be to bring the things you desire to you and to group them around you. So long as you hold your thought and your faith right all must go well. Nothing can be wrong but your own personal attitude, and that will not be wrong if you trust and are not afraid. Hurry is a manifestation of fear; he who fears not has plenty of time. If you act with perfect faith in your own perceptions of truth, you will never be too late or too early; and nothing will go wrong. If things appear to be going wrong, do not get disturbed in mind; it is only in appearance. Nothing can go wrong in this world but yourself; and you can go wrong only by getting into the wrong mental attitude. Whenever you find yourself getting excited, worried, or into the mental attitude of hurry, sit down and think it over, play a game of some kind, or take a vacation. Go on a trip, and all will be right when you return. So surely as you find yourself in the mental attitude of haste, just so surely may you know that you are out of the mental attitude of greatness. Hurry and fear will instantly cut your connection with the universal mind; you will get no power, no wisdom, and no information until you are calm. And to fall into the attitude of hurry will check the action of the Principle of Power within you. Fear turns strength to weakness.

Remember that poise and power are inseparably associated.

The calm and balanced mind is the strong and great mind; the hurried and agitated mind is the weak one. Whenever you fall into the mental state of hurry you may know that you have lost the right viewpoint; you are beginning to look upon the world, or some part of it, as going wrong. At such times read Chapter Six of this book; consider the fact that this work is perfect, now, with all that it contains. Nothing is going wrong; nothing can be wrong; be poised, be calm, be cheerful; have faith in God.

Next as to habit, it is probable that your greatest difficulty will be to overcome your old habitual ways of thought, and to form new habits. The world is ruled by habit. Kings, tyrants, masters, and plutocrats hold their positions solely because the people have come to habitually accept them. Things are as they are only because people have formed the habit of accepting them as they are. When the people change their habitual thought about governmental, social, and industrial institutions, they will change the institutions.

Habit rules us all.

You have formed, perhaps, the habit of thinking of yourself as a common person, as one of a limited ability, or as being more or less of a failure. Whatever you habitually think yourself to be, that you are. You must form, now, a greater and better habit; you must form a conception of yourself as a being of limitless power, and habitually think that you are that being. It is the habitual, not the periodical thought that decides your destiny. It will avail you nothing to sit apart for a few moments several times a day to affirm that you are great, if during all the balance of the day, while you are about your regular vocation, you think of yourself as not great. No amount of praying or affirmation will make you great if you still habitually regard yourself as being small.

The use of prayer and affirmation is to change your habit of thought. Any act, mental or physical, often repeated, becomes a habit. The purpose of mental exercises is to repeat certain thoughts over and over until the thinking of those thoughts becomes constant and habitual. The thoughts we continually repeat become convictions. What you must do is to repeat the new thought of yourself until it is the only way in which you think of yourself. Habitual thought, and not environment or circumstance, has made you what you are. Every person has some central idea or thought-form of himself, and by this idea he classifies and arranges all his facts and external relationships. You are classifying your facts either according to the idea that you are a great and strong personality, or according to the idea that you are limited, common, or weak. If the latter is the case you must change your central idea.

Get a new mental picture of yourself. Do not try to become great by repeating mere strings of words or superficial formulas; but repeat over and over the THOUGHT of your own power and ability until you classify external facts, and decide your place everywhere by this idea. In another chapter will be found an illustrative mental exercise and further directions on this point.

Chapter 13
Thought

GREATNESS is only attained by the constant thinking of great thoughts. No man can become great in outward personality until he is great internally; and no man can be great internally until he THINKS. No amount of education, reading, or study can make you great without thought; but thought can make you great with very little study. There are altogether too many people who are trying to make something of themselves, by reading books without thinking; all such will fail. You are not mentally developed by what you read, but by what you think about what you read.

Thinking is the hardest and most exhausting of all labor; and hence many people shrink from it. God has so formed us that we are continuously impelled to thought; we must either think or engage in some activity to escape thought. The headlong, continuous chase for pleasure in which most people spend all their leisure time is only an effort to escape thought. If they are alone, or if they have nothing amusing to take their attention, as a novel to read or a show to see, they must think; and to escape from thinking they resort to novels, shows, and all the endless devices of the purveyors of amusement. Most people spend the greater part of their leisure time running away from thought, hence they are where they are. We never move forward until we begin to think.

Read less and think more. Read about great things and think about great questions and issues. We have at the present time few really great figures in the political life of our country; our politicians are a petty lot. There is no Lincoln, no Webster, no Clay, Calhoun, or Jackson. Why? Because our present statesmen deal only with sordid and petty issues - questions of dollars and cents, of expediency and party success, of material prosperity without regard to ethical right. Thinking along these lines does not call forth great souls. The statesmen of Lincoln's time and previous times dealt with questions of eternal truth, of human rights and justice. Men thought upon great themes; they thought great thoughts, and they became great men.

Thinking, not mere knowledge or information, makes personality. Thinking is growth; you cannot think without growing.

Every thought engenders another thought. Write one idea and others will follow until you have written a page. You cannot fathom your own mind; it has neither bottom nor boundaries. Your first thoughts may be crude; but as you go on thinking you will use more and more of yourself; you will quicken new brain cells into activity and you will develop new faculties. Heredity, environment, circumstances, all things must give way before you if you practice sustained and continuous thought. But, on the other hand, if you neglect to think for yourself and only use other people's thought, you will never know what you are capable of; and you will end by being incapable of anything.

There can be no real greatness without original thought. All that a man does outwardly is the expression and completion of his inward thinking. No action is possible without thought, and no great action is possible until a great thought has preceded it. Action is the second form of thought, and personality is the materialization of thought. Environment is the result of thought; things group themselves or arrange themselves around you according to your thought. There is, as Emerson says, some central idea or conception of yourself by which all the facts of your life are arranged and classified. Change this central idea and you change the arrangement or classification of all the facts and circumstances of your life. You are what you are because you think as you do; you are where you are because you think as you do.

You see then the immense importance of thinking about the great essentials set forth in the preceding chapters. You must not accept them in any superficial way; you must think about them until they are a part of your central idea. Go back to the matter of the point of view and consider, in all its bearings, the tremendous thought that you live in a perfect world among perfect people, and that nothing can possibly be wrong with you but your own personal attitude. Think about all this until you fully realize all that it means to you. Consider that this is God's world and that it is the best of all possible worlds; that he has brought it thus far toward completion by the processes of organic, social, and industrial evolution, and that it is going on to greater completeness and harmony. Consider that there is one great, perfect, intelligent Principle of Life and Power, causing all the changing phenomena of the cosmos. Think about all this until you see that it is true, and until you comprehend how you should live and act as a citizen of such a perfect whole.

Next, think of the wonderful truth that this great Intelligence is in you; it is your own intelligence. It is an Inner Light impelling you toward the right thing and the best thing, the greatest act, and the highest happiness. It is a Principle of Power in you, giving you all the ability and genius there is. It will infallibly guide you to the best if you will submit to it and walk in the light. Consider what is meant by your consecration of yourself when you say: "I will obey my soul." This is a sentence of tremendous meaning; it must revolutionize the attitude and behavior of the average person. Then think of your identification with this Great Supreme; that all its knowledge is yours, and all its wisdom is yours, for the asking. You are a god if you think like a god. If you think like a god you cannot fail to act like a god. Divine thoughts will surely externalize themselves in a divine life. Thoughts of power will end in a life of power. Great thoughts will manifest in a great personality.

Think well of all this, and then you are ready to act.

Chapter 14
Action at Home

DO not merely think that you are going to become great; think that you are great now. Do not think that you will begin to act in a great way at some future time; begin now. Do not think that you will act in a great way when you reach a different environment; act in a great way where you are now. Do not think that you will begin to act in a great way when you begin to deal with great things; begin to deal in a great way with small things. Do not think that you will begin to be great when you get among more intelligent people, or among people who understand you better; begin now to deal in a great way with the people around you.

If you are not in an environment where there is scope for your best powers and talents you can move in due time; but meanwhile you can be great where you are. Lincoln was as great when he was a backwoods lawyer as when he was President; as a backwoods lawyer he did common things in a great way, and that made him President. Had he waited until he reached Washington to begin to be great, he would have remained unknown. You are not made great by the location in which you happen to be nor by the things with which you may surround yourself. You are not made great by what you receive from others, and you can never manifest greatness so long as you depend on others. You will manifest greatness only when you begin to stand alone. Dismiss all thought of reliance on externals, whether things, books, or people. As Emerson said, "Shakespeare will never be made by the study of Shakespeare." Shakespeare will be made by the thinking of Shakespearean thoughts.

Never mind how the people around you, including those of your own household, may treat you. That has nothing at all to do with your being great; that is, it cannot hinder you from being great. People may neglect you and be unthankful and unkind in their attitude toward you; does that prevent you from being great in your manner and attitude toward them? "Your Father," said Jesus, "is kind to the unthankful and the evil." Would God be great if he should go away and sulk because people were unthankful and did not appreciate him? Treat the unthankful and the evil in a great and perfectly kind way, just as God does. Do not talk about your greatness; you are really, in essential nature, no greater than those around you. You may have entered upon a way of living and thinking which they have not yet found, but they are perfect on their own plane of thought and action. You are entitled to no special honor or consideration for your greatness.

You are a god, but you are among gods. You will fall into the boastful attitude if you see other people's shortcomings and failures and compare them with your own virtues and successes; and if you fall into the boastful attitude of mind, you will cease to be great, and become small. Think of yourself as a perfect being among perfect beings, and meet every person as an equal, not as either superior or an inferior. Give yourself no airs; great people never do. Ask no honors and seek for no recognition, honors and recognition will come fast enough if you are entitled to them.

Begin at home. It is a great person who can always be poised, assured, calm, and perfectly kind and considerate at home. If your manner and attitude in your own family are always the best you can think, you will soon become the one on whom all the others will rely. You will be a tower of strength and a support in time of trouble. You will be loved and appreciated. At the same time do not make the mistake of throwing yourself away in the service of others. The great person respects himself; he serves and helps, but he is never slavishly servile. You cannot help your family by being a slave to them, or by doing for them those things that by right they should do for themselves. You do a person an injury when you wait on him too much. The selfish and exacting are a great deal better off if their exactions are denied. The ideal world is not one where there are a lot of people being waited on by other people; it is a world where everybody waits on himself. Meet all demands, selfish and otherwise, with perfect kindness and consideration; but do not allow yourself to be made a slave to the whims, caprices, exactions, or slavish desires of any member of your family. To do so is not great, and it works an injury to the other party.

Do not become uneasy over the failures or mistakes of any member of your family, and feel that you must interfere. Do not be disturbed if others seem to be going wrong, and feel that you must step in and set them right. Remember that every person is perfect on his own plane; you cannot improve on the work of God. Do not meddle with the personal habits and practices of others, though they are your nearest and dearest; these things are none of your business. Nothing can be wrong but your own personal attitude; make that right and you will know that all else is right. You are a truly great soul when you can live with those who do things that you do not do, and yet refrain from either criticism or interference.

Do the things that are right for you to do, and believe that every member of your family is doing the things that are right for him.

Nothing is wrong with anybody or anything, behold, it is all very good. Do not be enslaved by anyone else, but be just as careful that you do not enslave anyone else to your own notions of what is right. Think, and think deeply and continuously; be perfect in your kindness and consideration; let your attitude be that of a god among gods, and not that of a god among inferior beings. This is the way to be great in your own home.

Chapter 15
Action Abroad

THE rules that apply to your action at home must apply to your action everywhere. Never forget for an instant that this is a perfect world, and that you are a god among gods. You are as great as the greatest, but all are your equals.

Rely absolutely on your perception of truth. Trust to the inner light rather than to reason, but be sure that your perception comes from the inner light; act in poise and calmness; be still and attend on God. Your identification of yourself with the All-Mind will give you all the knowledge you need for guidance in any contingency that may arise in your own life or in the lives of others. It is only necessary that you should be supremely calm, and rely upon the eternal wisdom that is within you. If you act in poise and faith, your judgment will always be right, and you will always know exactly what to do. Do not hurry or worry; remember Lincoln in the dark days of the war. James Freeman Clarke relates that after the battle of Fredericksburg, Lincoln alone furnished a supply of faith and hope for the nation. Hundreds of leading men, from all parts of the country, went sadly into his room and came out cheerful and hopeful. They had stood face to face with the Highest, and had seen God in this lank, ungainly, patient man, although they knew it not.

Have perfect faith in yourself and in your own ability to cope with any combination of circumstances that may arise. Do not be disturbed if you are alone; if you need friends they will be brought to you at the right time. Do not be disturbed if you feel that you are ignorant, the information that you need will be furnished you when it is time for you to have it. That which is in you impelling you forward is in the things and people you need, impelling them toward you. If there is a particular man you need to know, he will be introduced to you; if there is a particular book you need to read it will be placed in your hands at the right time. All the knowledge you need is coming to you from both external and internal sources. Your information and your talents will always be equal to the requirements of the occasion. Remember that Jesus told his disciples not to worry as to what they should say when brought before the judges; he knew that the power in them would be sufficient for the needs of the hour. As soon as you awaken and begin to use your faculties in a great way you will apply power to the development of your brain; new cells will be created and dormant cells quickened into activity, and your brain will be qualified as a perfect instrument for your mind.

Do not try to do great things until you are ready to go about them in a great way. If you undertake to deal with great matters in a small way — that is, from a low viewpoint or with incomplete consecration and wavering faith and courage — you will fail. Do not be in a hurry to get to the great things. Doing great things will not make you great, but becoming great will certainly lead you to the doing of great things. Begin to be great where you are and in the things you do every day. Do not be in haste to be found out or recognized as a great personality. Do not be disappointed if men do not nominate you for office within a month after you begin to practice what you read in this book. Great people never seek for recognition or applause; they are not great because they want to be paid for being so. Greatness is reward enough for itself; the joy of being something and of knowing that you are advancing is the greatest of all joys possible to man.

If you begin in your own family, as described in the preceding chapter, and then assume the same mental attitude with your neighbors, friends, and those you meet in business, you will soon find that people are beginning to depend on you. Your advice will be sought, and a constantly increasing number of people will look to you for strength and inspiration, and rely upon your judgment.

Here, as in the home, you must avoid meddling with other people's affairs. Help all who come to you, but do not go about officiously endeavoring to set other people right. Mind your own business. It is no part of your mission in life to correct people's morals, habits, or practices. Lead a great life, doing all things with a great spirit and in a great way; give to him that asks of you as freely as you have received, but do not force your help or your opinions upon any man. If your neighbor wishes to smoke or drink, it is his business; it is none of yours until he consults you about it. If you lead a great life and do no preaching, you will save a thousand times as many souls as one who leads a small life and preaches continuously.

If you hold the right viewpoint of the world, others will find it out and be impressed by it through your daily conversation and practice. Do not try to convert others to your point of view, except by holding it and living accordingly. If your consecration is perfect you do not need to tell anyone; it will speedily become apparent to all that you are guided by a higher principle than the average man or woman. If your identification with God is complete, you do not need to explain the fact to others; it will become self-evident. To become known as a great personality, you have nothing to do but to live. Do not imagine that you must go charging about the world like Don Quixote, tilting at windmills, and overturning things in general, in order to demonstrate that you are somebody. Do not go hunting for big things to do. Live a great life where you are, and in the daily work you have to do, and greater works will surely find you out. Big things will come to you, asking to be done.

Be so impressed with the value of a man that you treat even a beggar or the tramp with the most distinguished consideration. All is God. Every man and woman is perfect. Let your manner be that of a god addressing other gods. Do not save all your consideration for the poor; the millionaire is as good as the tramp. This is a perfectly good world, and there is not a person or thing in it but is exactly right; be sure that you keep this in mind in dealing with things and men.

Form your mental vision of yourself with care. Make the thought-form of yourself as you wish to be, and hold this with the faith that it is being realized, and with the purpose to realize it completely. Do every common act as a god should do it; speak every word as a god should speak it; meet men and women of both low and high estate as a god meets other divine beings. Begin thus and continue thus, and your unfolding in ability and power will be great and rapid.

Chapter 16
Some Further Explanations

WE go back here to the matter of the point of view, for, besides being vitally important, it is the one that is likely to give the student the most trouble. We have been trained, partly by mistaken religious teachers, to look upon the world as being like a wrecked ship, storm-driven upon a rocky coast; utter destruction is inevitable at the end, and the most that can be done is to rescue, perhaps, a few of the crew. This view teaches us to consider the world as essentially bad and growing worse; and to believe that existing discords and inharmoniousness must continue and intensify until the end. It robs us of hope for society, government, and humanity, and gives us a decreasing outlook and contracting mind.

This is all wrong. The world is not wrecked. It is like a magnificent steamer with the engines in place and the machinery in perfect order. The bunkers are full of coal, and the ship is amply provisioned for the cruise; there is no lack of any good thing. Every provision Omniscience could devise has been made for the safety, comfort, and happiness of the crew; the steamer is out on the high seas tacking hither and thither because no one has yet learned the right course to steer. We are learning to steer, an in due time will come grandly into the harbor of perfect harmony.

The world is good, and growing better. Existing discords and inharmoniousness are but the pitching of the ship incidental to our own imperfect steering; they will all be removed in due time. This view gives us an increasing outlook and an expanding mind; it enables us to think largely of society and of ourselves, and to do things in a great way.

Furthermore, we see that nothing can be wrong with such a world or with any part of it, including our own affairs. If it is all moving on toward completion, then it is not going wrong; and as our own personal affairs are a part of the whole, they are not going wrong. You and all that you are concerned with are moving on toward completeness. Nothing can check this forward movement but yourself; and you can only check it by assuming a mental attitude that is at cross-purposes with the mind of God. You have nothing to keep right but yourself; if you keep yourself right, nothing can possibly go wrong with you, and you can have nothing to fear. No business or other disaster can come upon you if your personal attitude is right, for you are a part of that which is increasing and advancing, and you must increase and advance with it.

Moreover your thought-form will be mostly shaped according to your viewpoint of the cosmos. If you see the world as a lost and ruined thing you will see yourself as a part of it, and as partaking of its sins and weaknesses. If your outlook for the world as a whole is hopeless, your outlook for yourself cannot be hopeful. If you see the world as declining toward its end, you cannot see yourself as advancing. Unless you think well of all the works of God you cannot really think well of yourself, and unless you think well of yourself you can never become great.

I repeat that your place in life, including your material environment, is determined by the thought-form you habitually hold of yourself. When you make a thought-form of yourself you can hardly fail to form in your mind a corresponding environment. If you think of yourself as an incapable, inefficient person, you will think of yourself with poor or cheap surroundings. Unless you think well of yourself you will be sure to picture yourself in a more or less poverty stricken environment. These thoughts, habitually held, become invisible forms in the surrounding mind-stuff, and are with you continually. In due time, by the regular action of the eternal creative energy, the invisible thought-forms are produced in material stuff, and you are surrounded by your own thoughts made into material things.

See nature as a great living and advancing presence, and see human society in exactly the same way. It is all one, coming from one source, and it is all good. You yourself are made of the same stuff as God. All the constituents of God are parts of you; every power that God has is a constituent of man. You can move forward as you see God doing. You have within yourself the source of every power.

Chapter 17
More About Thought

GIVE place here to some further consideration of thought. You will never become great until your own thoughts make you great, and therefore it is of the first importance that you should THINK.

You will never do great things in the external world until you think great things in the internal world; and you will never think great things until you think about truth; about the verities. To think great things you must be absolutely sincere; and to be sincere you must know that your intentions are right. Insincere or false thinking is never great, however logical and brilliant it may be.

The first and most important step is to seek the truth about human relations, to know what you ought to be to other men, and what they ought to be to you. This brings you back to the search for a right viewpoint. You should study organic and social evolution.

Read Darwin and Walter Thomas Mills, and when you read, THINK; think the whole matter over until you see the world of things and men in the right way. THINK about what God is doing until you can SEE what he is doing.

Your next step is to think yourself into the right personal attitude. Your viewpoint tells you what the right attitude is, and obedience to the soul puts you into it. It is only by making a complete consecration of yourself to the highest that is within you that you can attain to sincere thinking. So long as you know you are selfish in your aims, or dishonest or crooked in any way in your intentions or practices, your thinking will be false and your thoughts will have no power. THINK about the way you are doing things; about all your intentions, purposes, and practices, until you know that they are right.

The fact of his own complete unity with God is one that no person can grasp without deep and sustained thinking. Anyone can accept the proposition in a superficial way, but to feel and realize a vital comprehension of it is another matter. It is easy to think of going outside of yourself to meet God, but it is not so easy to think of going inside yourself to meet God. But God is there, and in the holy of holies of your own soul you may meet him face to face. It is a tremendous thing; this fact that all you need is already within you; that you do not have to consider how to get the power to do what you want to do or to make yourself what you want to be.

You have only to consider how to use the power you have in the right way. And there is nothing to do but to begin. Use your perception of truth; you can see some truth today; live fully up to that and you will see more truth tomorrow.

To rid yourself of the old false ideas you will have to think a great deal about the value of men — the greatness and worth of a human soul. You must cease from looking at human mistakes and look at successes; cease from seeing faults and see virtues. You can no longer look upon men and women as lost and ruined beings that are descending into hell; you must come to regard them as shining souls who are ascending toward heaven. It will require some exercise of will power to do this, but this is the legitimate use of the will — to decide what you will think about and how you will think.

The function of the will is to direct thought. Think about the good side of men; the lovely, attractive part, and exert your will in refusing to think of anything else in connection with them.

I know of no one who has attained to so much on this one point as Eugene V. Debs, twice the Socialist candidate for president of the United States. Mr. Debs reverences humanity. No appeal for help is ever made to him in vain. No one receives from him an unkind or censorious word. You cannot come into his presence without being made sensible of his deep and kindly personal interest in you. Every person, be he millionaire, grimy workingman, or toil worn woman, receives the radiant warmth of a brotherly affection that is sincere and true. No ragged child speaks to him on the street without receiving instant and tender recognition. Debs loves men. This has made him the leading figure in a great movement, the beloved hero of a million hearts, and will give him a deathless name. It is a great thing to love men so and it is only achieved by thought. No thing can make you great but thought.

"We may divide thinkers into those who think for themselves and those who think through others. The latter are the rule and the former the exception. The first are original thinkers in a double sense, and egotists in the noblest meaning of the word." —Sehopenhauer

"The key to every man is his thought. Sturdy and defiant though he look he has a helm which he obeys, which is the idea after which all his facts are classified. He can only be reformed by showing him a new idea which commands his own." —Emerson

"All truly wise thoughts have been thought already thousands of times; but to make them really ours we must think them over again honestly till they take root in our personal expression." —Goethe

"All that a man is outwardly is but the expression and completion of his inward thought. To work effectively he must think clearly. To act nobly he must think nobly." —Channing

"Great men are they who see that spirituality is stronger than any material force; that thoughts rule the world." —Emerson

"Some people study all their lives, and at their death they have learned everything except to think." —Domergue

"It is the habitual thought that frames itself into our life. It affects us even more than our intimate social relations do. Our confidential friends have not so much to do in shaping our lives as the thoughts have which we harbor." —J. W. Teal

"When God lets loose a great thinker on this planet, then all things are at risk. There is not a piece of science but its flank may be turned tomorrow; nor any literary reputation or the so-called eternal names of fame that may not be refused and condemned." —Emerson

Think! Think!! THINK!!!

Chapter 18
Jesus' Idea of Greatness

IN the twenty-third chapter of Matthew, Jesus makes a very plain distinction between true and false greatness; and also points out the one great danger to all who wish to become great; the most insidious of temptations which all must avoid and fight unceasingly who desire to really climb in the world. Speaking to the multitude and to his disciples he bids them beware of adopting the principle of the Pharisees. He points out that while the Pharisees are just and righteous men, honorable judges, true lawgivers and upright in their dealings with men, they "love the uppermost seats at feasts and greetings in the market place, and to be called Master, Master"; and in comparison with this principle, he says: "He that will be great among you let him serve."

The average person's idea of a great man, rather than of one who serves, is of one who succeeds in getting himself served. He gets himself in a position to command men; to exercise power over them, making them obey his will. The exercise of dominion over other people, to most persons, is a great thing. Nothing seems to be sweeter to the selfish soul than this. You will always find every selfish and undeveloped person trying to domineer over others, to exercise control over other men. Savage men were no sooner placed upon the earth than they began to enslave one another. For ages the struggle in war, diplomacy, politics, and government has been aimed at the securing of control over other men. Kings and princes have drenched the soil of the earth in blood and tears in the effort to extend their dominions and their power to rule more people.

The struggle of the business world today is the same as that on the battlefields of Europe a century ago so far as the ruling principle is concerned. Robert O. Ingersoll could not understand why men like Rockefeller and Carnegie seek for more money and make themselves slaves to the business struggle when they already have more than they can possibly use. He thought it a kind of madness and illustrated it as follows: "Suppose a man had fifty thousand pairs of pants, seventy-five thousand vests, one hundred thousand coats, and one hundred and fifty thousand neckties, what would you think of him if he arose in the morning before light and worked until after it was dark every day, rain or shine, in all kinds of weather, merely to get another necktie?"

But it is not a good simile. The possession of neckties gives a man no power over other men, while the possession of dollars does. Rockefeller, Carnegie, and their kind are not after dollars but power. It is the principle of the Pharisee; it is the struggle for the high place. It develops able men, cunning men, resourceful men, but not great men.

I want you to contrast these two ideas of greatness sharply in your minds. "He that will be great among you let him serve." Let me stand before the average American audience and ask the name of the greatest American and the majority will think of Abraham Lincoln; and is this not because in Lincoln above all the other men who have served us in public life we recognize the spirit of service? Not servility, but service. Lincoln was a great man because he knew how to be a great servant. Napoleon, able, cold, selfish, seeking the high places, was a brilliant man. Lincoln was great; Napoleon was not. The very moment you begin to advance and are recognized as one who is doing things in a great way you will find yourself in danger. The temptation to patronize, advise, or take upon yourself the direction of other people's affairs is sometimes almost irresistible. Avoid, however, the opposite danger of falling into servility, or of completely throwing yourself away in the service of others. To do this has been the ideal of a great many people. The completely self-sacrificing life has been thought to be the Christ-like life, because, as I think, of a complete misconception of the character and teachings of Jesus. I have explained this misconception in a little book that I hope you may all sometime read, "A New Christ". Thousands of people imitating Jesus, as they suppose, have belittled themselves and given up all else to go about doing good; practicing an altruism that is really as morbid and as far from great as the rankest selfishness. The finer instincts which respond to the cry of trouble or distress are not by any means all of you; they are not necessarily the best part of you. There are other things you must do besides helping the unfortunate, although it is true that a large part of the life and activities of every great person must be given to helping other people. As you begin to advance they will come to you. Do not turn them away. But do not make the fatal error of supposing that the life of complete self-abnegation is the way of greatness.

To make another point here, let me refer to the fact that Swedenborg's classification of fundamental motives is exactly the same as that of Jesus. He divides all men into two groups: those who live in pure love, and those who live in what he calls the love of ruling for the love of self. It will be seen that this is exactly the same as the lust for place and power of the Pharisees. Swedenborg saw this selfish love of power as the cause of all sin. It was the only evil desire of the human heart, from which all other evil desires sprang.

Over against this he places pure love. He does not say love of God or love of man, but merely love. Nearly all religionists make more of love and service to God than they do of love and service to man. But it is a fact that love to God is not sufficient to save a man from the lust for power, for some of the most ardent lovers of the Deity have been the worst of tyrants. Lovers of God are often tyrants, and lovers of men are often meddlesome and officious.

Chapter 19
A View of Evolution

BUT how shall we avoid throwing ourselves into altruistic work if we are surrounded by poverty, ignorance, suffering, and every appearance of misery as very many people are? Those who live where the withered hand of want is thrust upon them from every side appealingly for aid must find it hard to refrain from continuous giving. Again, there are social and other irregularities, injustices done to the weak, which fire generous souls with an almost irresistible desire to set things right. We want to start a crusade; we feel that the wrongs will never be righted until we give ourselves wholly to the task. In all this we must fall back upon the point of view. We must remember that this is not a bad world but a good world in the process of becoming.

Beyond all doubt there was a time when there was no life upon this earth. The testimony of geology to the fact that the globe was once a ball of burning gas and molten rock, clothed about with boiling vapors, is indisputable. And we do not know how life could have existed under such conditions; that seems impossible. Geology tells us that later on a crust formed, the globe cooled and hardened, the vapors condensed and became mist or fell in rain. The cooled surface crumbled into soil; moisture accumulated, ponds and seas were gathered together, and at last somewhere in the water or on the land appeared something that was alive.

It is reasonable to suppose that this first life was in single-celled organisms, but behind these cells was the insistent urge of Spirit, the Great One Life seeking expression. And soon organisms having too much life to express themselves with one cell had two cells and then many, and still more life was poured into them.

Multiple-celled organisms were formed; plants, trees, vertebrates, and mammals, many of them with strange shapes, but all were perfect after their kind as everything is that God makes. No doubt there were crude and almost monstrous forms of both animal and plant life; but everything filled its purpose in its day and it was all very good. Then another day came, the great day of the evolutionary process, a day when the morning stars sang together and the sons of God shouted for joy to behold the beginning of the end, for man, the object aimed at from the beginning, had appeared upon the scene. An ape-like being, little different from the beasts around him in appearance, but infinitely different capacity for growth and thought. Art and beauty, architecture and song, poetry and music, all these were unrealized possibilities in that ape man's soul. And for his time and kind he was very good.

"It is God that works in you to will and to do of his good pleasure," says St. Paul. From the day the first man appeared God began to work IN men, putting more and more of himself into each succeeding generation, urging them on to larger achievements and to better conditions, social, governmental, and domestic. Those who looking back into ancient history see the awful conditions which existed, the barbarities, idolatries, and sufferings, and reading about God in connection with these things are disposed to feel that he was cruel and unjust to man, should pause to think. From the ape-man to the coming Christ man the race has had to rise. And it could only be accomplished by the successive unfolding of the various powers and possibilities latent in the human brain.

God desired to express himself, to live in form, and not only that, but to live in a form through which he could express himself on the highest moral and spiritual plane. God wanted to evolve a form in which he could live as a god and manifest himself as a god. This was the aim of the evolutionary force. The ages of warfare, bloodshed, suffering, injustice, and cruelty were tempered in many ways with love and justice as time advanced. And this was developing the brain of man to a point where it should be capable of giving full expression to the love and justice of God. The end is not yet; God aims not at the perfection of a few choice specimens for exhibition, like the large berries at the top of the box, but at the glorification of the race. The time will come when the Kingdom of God shall be established on earth; the time foreseen by the dreamer of the Isle of Patmos, when there shall be no more crying, neither shall there be any more pain, for the former things are all passed away, and there shall be no night there.

Chapter 20
Serving God

I HAVE brought you thus far through the two preceding chapters with a view to finally settling the question of duty. This is one that puzzles and perplexes very many people who are earnest and sincere, and gives them a great deal of difficulty in its solution.

When they start out to make something of themselves and to practice the science of being great, they find themselves necessarily compelled to rearrange many of their relationships. There are friends who perhaps must be alienated, there are relatives who misunderstand and who feel that they are in some way being slighted; the really great man is often considered selfish by a large circle of people who are connected with him and who feel that he might bestow upon them more benefits than he does. The question at the outset is: Is it my duty to make the most of myself regardless of everything else? Or shall I wait until I can do so without any friction or without causing loss to any one? This is the question of duty to self vs. duty to others.

One's duty to the world has been thoroughly discussed in the preceding pages and I give some consideration now to the idea of duty to God. An immense number of people have a great deal of uncertainty, not to say anxiety, as to what they ought to do for God.

The amount of work and service that is done for him in these United States in the way of church work and so on is enormous. An immense amount of human energy is expended in what is called serving God. I propose to consider briefly what serving God is and how a man may serve God best, and I think I shall be able to make plain that the conventional idea as to what constitutes service to God is all wrong.

When Moses went down into Egypt to bring out the Hebrews from bondage, his demand upon Pharaoh, in the name of the Deity, was, "Let the people go that they may serve me." He led them out into the wilderness and there instituted a new form of worship which has led many people to suppose that worship constitutes the service of God, although later God himself distinctly declared that he cared nothing for ceremonies, burned offerings, or oblation, and the teaching of Jesus if rightly understood, would do away with organized temple worship altogether. God does not lack anything that men may do for him with their hands or bodies or voices. Saint Paul points out that man can do no thing for God, for God does not need anything.

The view of evolution that we have taken shows God seeking expression through man. Through all the successive ages in which his spirit has urged man up the height, God has gone on seeking expression. Every generation of men is more Godlike than the preceding generation. Every generation of men demands more in the way of fine homes, pleasant surroundings, congenial work, rest, travel, and opportunity for study than the preceding generation.

I have heard some shortsighted economists argue that the working people of today ought surely to be fully contented because their condition is so much better than that of the workingman two hundred years ago who slept in a windowless hut on a floor covered with rushes in company with his pigs. If that man had all that he was able to use for the living of all the life he knew how to live, he was perfectly content, and if he had lack he was not contented. The man of today has a comfortable home and very many things, indeed, that were unknown a short period back in the past, and if he has all that he can use for the living of all the life he can imagine, he will be content. But he is not content. God has lifted the race so far that any common man can picture a better and more desirable life than he is able to live under existing conditions. And so long as this is true, so long as a man can think and clearly picture to himself a more desirable life, he will be discontented with the life he has to live, and rightly so. That discontent is the Spirit of God urging men on to more desirable conditions. It is God who seeks expression in the race. "He works in us to will and to do."

The only service you can render God is to give expression to what he is trying to give the world, through you. The only service you can render God is to make the very most of yourself in order that God may live in you to the utmost of your possibilities. In a former work of this series (The Science of Getting Rich) I refer to the little boy at the piano, the music in whose soul could not find expression through his untrained hands. This is a good illustration of the way the Spirit of God is over, about, around, and in all of us, seeking to do great things with us, so soon as we will train our hands and feet, our minds, brains, and bodies to do his service.

Your first duty to God, to yourself, and to the world is to make yourself as great a personality, in every way, as you possibly can. And that, it seems to me, disposes of the question of duty. There are one or two other things that might be disposed of in closing this chapter. I have written of opportunity in a preceding chapter. I have said, in a general way, that it is within the power of every man to become great, just as in "The Science of Getting Rich" I declared that it is within the power of every man to become rich. But these sweeping generalizations need qualifying. There are men who have such materialistic minds that they are absolutely incapable of comprehending the philosophy set forth in these books. There is a great mass of men and women who have lived and worked until they are practically incapable of thought along these lines; and they cannot receive the message. Something may be done for them by demonstration, that is, by living the life before them. But that is the only way they can be aroused. The world needs demonstration more than it needs teaching. For this mass of people our duty is to become as great in personality as possible in order that they may see and desire to do likewise. It is our duty to make ourselves great for their sakes; so that we may help prepare the world that the next generation shall have better conditions for thought.

One other point; I am frequently written to by people who wish to make something of themselves and to move out into the world, but who are hampered by home ties, having others more or less dependent upon them, whom they fear would suffer if left alone. In general I advise such people to move out fearlessly, and to make the most of themselves. If there is a loss at home it will be only temporary and apparent, for in a little while, if you follow the leading of Spirit, you will be able to take better care of your dependents than you have ever done before.

Chapter 21
A Mental Exercise

THE purpose of mental exercises must not be misunderstood. There is no virtue in charms or formulated strings of words; there is no short cut to development by repeating prayers or incantations. A mental exercise is an exercise, not in repeating words, but in the thinking of certain thoughts. The phrases that we repeatedly hear become convictions, as Goethe says; and the thoughts that we repeatedly think become habitual, and make us what we are. The purpose in taking a mental exercise is that you may think certain thoughts repeatedly until you form a habit of thinking them; then they will be your thoughts all the time. Taken in the right way and with an understanding of their purpose, mental exercises are of great value; but taken as most people take them they are worse than useless.

The thoughts embodied in the following exercise are the ones you want to think. You should take the exercise once or twice daily, but you should think the thoughts continuously. That is, do not think them twice a day for a stated time and then forget them until it is time to take the exercise again. The exercise is to impress you with the material for continuous thought.

Take a time when you can have from twenty minutes to half an hour secure from interruption, and proceed first to make yourself physically comfortable. Lie at ease in a Morris chair, or on a couch, or in bed; it is best to lie flat on your back. If you have no other time, take the exercise on going to bed at night and before rising in the morning.

First let your attention travel over your body from the crown of your head to the soles of your feet, relaxing every muscle as you go.

Relax completely. And next, get physical and other ills off your mind. Let the attention pass down the spinal cord and out over the nerves to the extremities, and as you do so think: "My nerves are in perfect order all over my body. They obey my will, and I have great nerve force." Next bring your attention to the lungs and think: "I am breathing deeply and quietly, and the air goes into every cell of my lungs, which are in perfect condition. My blood is purified and made clean." Next, to the heart: "My heart is beating strongly and steadily, and my circulation is perfect, even to the extremities." Next, to the digestive system: "My stomach and bowels perform their work perfectly. My food is digested and assimilated and my body rebuilt and nourished. My liver, kidneys, and bladder each perform their several functions without pain or strain; I am perfectly well. My body is resting, my mind is quiet, and my soul is at peace.

"I have no anxiety about financial or other matters. God, who is within me, is also in all things I want, impelling them toward me; all that I want is already given to me. I have no anxiety about my health, for I am perfectly well. I have no worry or fear whatever.

"I rise above all temptation to moral evil. I cast out all greed, selfishness, and narrow personal ambition; I do not hold envy, malice, or enmity toward any living soul. I will follow no course of action which is not in accord with my highest ideals. I am right and I will do right."

VIEWPOINT

"All is right with the world. It is perfect and advancing to completion. I will contemplate the facts of social, political, and industrial life only from this high viewpoint. Behold, it is all very good. I will see all human beings, all my acquaintances, friends, neighbors, and the members of my own household in the same way. They are all good. Nothing is wrong with the universe; nothing can be wrong but my own personal attitude, and henceforth I keep that right. My whole trust is in God."

CONSECRATION

"I will obey my soul and be true to that within me that is highest. I will search within for the pure idea of right in all things, and when I find it I will express it in my outward life. I will abandon everything I have outgrown for the best I can think. I will have the highest thoughts concerning all my relationships, and my manner and action shall express these thoughts. I surrender my body to be ruled by my mind; I yield my mind to the dominion of my soul, and I give my soul to the guidance of God."

IDENTIFICATION

"There is but one substance and source, and of that I am made and with it I am one. It is my Father; I proceeded forth and came from it. My Father and I are one, and my Father is greater than I, and I do His will. I surrender myself to conscious unity with Pure Spirit; there is but one and that one is everywhere. I am one with the Eternal Consciousness."

IDEALIZATION

Form a mental picture of yourself as you want to be, and at the greatest height your imagination can picture. Dwell upon this for some little time, holding the thought: "This is what I really am; it is a picture of my own perfect and advancing to completion. I will contemplate the facts of social, political, and industrial life only from this high viewpoint. Behold, it is all very good. I will see all human beings, all my acquaintances, friends, neighbors, and the members of my own household in the same way. They are all good.

"Nothing is wrong with the universe, nothing can he wrong but my own personal attitude, and henceforth I keep that right. My whole trust is in God."

REALIZATION

"I appropriate to myself the power to become what I want to be, and to do what I want to do. I exercise creative energy; all the power there is, is mine.

I will arise and go forth with power and perfect confidence; I will do mighty works in the strength of the Lord, my God. I will trust and not fear, for God is with me."

Chapter 22
A Summary of The Science of Being Great

ALL men are made of the one intelligent substance, and therefore all contain the same essential powers and possibilities. Greatness is equally inherent in all, and may be manifested by all. Every person may become great. Every constituent of God is a constituent of man.

Man may overcome both heredity and circumstances by exercising the inherent creative power of the soul. If he is to become great, the soul must act, and must rule the mind and the body.

Man's knowledge is limited, and he falls into error through ignorance; to avoid this he must connect his soul with Universal Spirit. Universal Spirit is the intelligent substance from which all things come; it is in and through all things. All things are known to this universal mind, and man can so unite himself with it as to enter into all knowledge.

To do this man must cast out of himself everything that separates him from God. He must will to live the divine life, and he must rise above all moral temptations; he must forsake every course of action that is not in accord with his highest ideals.

He must reach the right viewpoint, recognizing that God is all, in all, and that there is nothing wrong. He must see that nature, society, government, and industry are perfect in their present stage, and advancing toward completion; and that all men and women everywhere are good and perfect. He must know that all is right with the world, and unite with God for the completion of the perfect work. It is only as man sees God as the Great Advancing Presence in all, and good in all that he can rise to real greatness.

He must consecrate himself to the service of the highest that is within himself, obeying the voice of the soul. There is an Inner Light in every man that continuously impels him toward the highest, and he must be guided by this light if he would become great.

He must recognize the fact that he is one with the Father, and consciously affirm this unity for himself and for all others. He must know himself to be a god among gods, and act accordingly. He must have absolute faith in his own perceptions of truth, and begin at home to act upon these perceptions. As he sees the true and right course in small things, he must take that course. He must cease to act unthinkingly, and begin to think; and he must be sincere in his thought.

He must form a mental conception of himself at the highest, and hold this conception until it is his habitual thought-form of himself. This thought-form he must keep continuously in view. He must outwardly realize and express that thought-form in his actions. He must do everything that he does in a great way. In dealing with his family, his neighbors, acquaintances, and friends, he must make every act an expression of his ideal. The man who reaches the right viewpoint and makes full consecration, and who fully idealizes himself as great, and who makes every act, however trivial, an expression of the ideal, has already attained to greatness. Everything he does will be done in a great way. He will make himself known, and will be recognized as a personality of power. He will receive knowledge by inspiration, and will know all that he needs to know. He will receive all the material wealth he forms in his thoughts, and will not lack for any good thing. He will be given ability to deal with any combination of circumstances that may arise, and his growth and progress will be continuous and rapid.

Great works will seek him out, and all men will delight to do him honor. Because of its peculiar value to the student of the Science of Being Great, I close this book by giving a portion of Emerson's essay on the "Oversoul." This great essay is fundamental, showing the foundation principles of monism and the science of greatness. I recommend the student to study it most carefully in connection with this book.

What is the universal sense of want and ignorance, but the fine innuendo by which the great soul makes its enormous claim? Why do men feel that the natural history of man has never been written, but always he is leaving behind what you have said of him, and it becomes old, and books of metaphysics worthless? The philosophy of six thousand years has not searched the chambers and magazines of the soul. In its experiments there has always remained, in the last analysis, a residuum it could not resolve. Man is a stream whose source is hidden. Always our being is descending into us from we know not whence. The most exact calculator has no prescience that somewhat incalculable may not balk the very next moment. I am constrained every moment to acknowledge a higher origin for events than the will I call mine.

As with events, so it is with thoughts. When I watch that flowing river, which, out of regions I see not, pours for a season its streams into me, I see that I am a pensioner, not a cause, but a surprised spectator of this ethereal water; that I desire and look up, and put myself in the attitude for reception, but from some alien energy the visions come.

The Supreme Critic on all the errors of the past and present, and the only prophet of that which must be, is that great nature in which we rest, as the earth lies in the soft arms of the atmosphere; that Unity, that Oversoul, with which every man's particular being is contained and made one with all other; that common heart, of which all sincere conversation is the worship, to which all right action is submission; that overpowering reality which confutes our tricks and talents, and constrains every one to pass for what he is, and to speak from his character and not from his tongue; and which evermore tends and aims to pass into our thought and hand, and become wisdom, and virtue, and power, and beauty. We live in succession, in division, in parts, in particles.

Meantime within man is the soul of the whole; the wise silence; the universal beauty, to which every part and particle is equally related, the eternal One. And this deep power in which we exist, and whose beatitude is all-accessible to us, is not only self sufficing and perfect in every hour, but the act of seeing, and the thing seen, the seer and the spectacle, the subject and the object, are one. We see the world piece by piece, as the sun, the moon, the animal, the tree; but the whole, of which these are the shining parts, is the soul. It is only by the vision of that Wisdom, that the horoscope of the ages can be read, and it is only by falling back on our better thoughts, by yielding to the spirit of prophecy which is innate in every man, that we know what it saith. Every man's words, who speaks from that life, must sound vain to those who do not dwell in the same thought on their own part. I dare not speak for it.

My words do not carry its august sense; they fall short and cold. Only itself can inspire whom it will, and behold! Their speech shall be lyrical and sweet, and universal as the rising of the wind.

Yet I desire, even by profane words, if sacred I may not use, to indicate the heaven of this deity, and to report what hints I have collected of the transcendent simplicity and energy of the Highest Law.

If we consider what happens in conversation, in reveries, in remorse, in times of passion, in surprises, in the instruction of dreams wherein often we see ourselves in masquerade, the droll disguises only magnifying and enhancing a real element, and forcing it on our distinct notice, we shall catch many hints that will broaden and lighten into knowledge of the secret of nature. All goes to show that the soul in man is not an organ, but animates and exercises all the organs; is not a function, like the power of memory, of calculation, of comparison, but uses these as hands and feet; is not a faculty, but a light; is not the intellect or the will, but the master of the intellect and the will; is the vast background of our being, in which they lie, an immensity not possessed and that cannot be possessed. From within or from behind, a light shines through us upon things, and makes us aware that we are nothing, but the light is all. A man is the facade of a temple wherein all wisdom and all good abide. What we commonly call man, the eating, drinking, planting, counting man, does not, as we know him, represent himself, but misrepresents himself. Him we do not respect, but the soul, whose organ he is, would he let it appear through his action, would make our knees bend. When it breathes through his intellect, it is genius; when it flows through his affection it is love.

After its own law and not by arithmetic is the rate of its progress to be computed. The soul's advances are not made by gradation, such as can be represented by motion in a straight line; but rather by ascension of state, such as can be represented by metamorphosis, from the egg to the worm, from the worm to the fly. The growths of genius are of a certain total character, that does not advance the elect individual first over John, then Adam, then Richard, and give to each the pain of discovered inferiority, but by every throe of growth the man expands there where he works, passing, at each pulsation, classes, populations of men. With each divine impulse the mind rends the thin rinds of the visible and finite, and comes out into eternity, and inspires and expires its air.

This is the law of moral and of mental gain. The simple rise, as by specific levity, not into a particular virtue, but into the region of all the virtues. They are in the spirit that contains them all. The soul is superior to all the particulars of merit. The soul requires purity, but purity is not it; requires justice, but justice is not that; requires beneficence, but is somewhat better; so that there is a kind of descent and accommodation felt when we leave speaking of moral nature, to urge a virtue which it enjoins. For, to the soul in her pure action, all the virtues are natural, and not painfully acquired. Speak to his heart and the man becomes suddenly virtuous. Within the same sentiment is the germ of intellectual growth, which obeys the same law. Those who are capable of humility, of justice, of love, of aspiration, are already on a platform that commands the sciences and arts, speech and poetry, action and grace. For who so dwells in this mortal beatitude, does already anticipate those special powers which men prize so highly; just as love does justice to all the gifts of the object beloved. The lover has no talent, no skill, which passes for quite nothing with his enamored maiden, however little she may possess of related faculty. And the heart that abandons itself to the Supreme Mind finds itself related to all its works and will travel a royal road to particular knowledge and powers. For, in ascending to this primary and aboriginal sentiment, we have come from our remote station on the circumference instantaneously to the center of the world, where, as in the closet of God, we see causes, and anticipate the universe, which is but a slow effect.

The Science of Being Well

by Wallace D. Wattles

edited by Jeffrey L. King

Contents

    Preface... 63
1. The Principle of Health............................ 64
2. The Foundation of Faith........................... 67
3. Life and Its Organisms 71
4. What to Think 74
5. Faith 78
6. Use of the Will 82
7. Health from God 85
8. Summary of the Mental Actions 88
9. When to Eat 90
10. What to Eat 93
11. How to Eat 96
12. Hunger and Appetites............................. 99
13. In a Nutshell..................................... 102
14. Breathing 105
15. Sleep 108
16. Supplementary Instructions 110
17. A Summary of The Science of Being Well............ 114

Preface

This volume is the second of a series, the first of which is "THE SCIENCE OF GETTING RICH." As that book is intended solely for those who want money, so this is for those who want health, and who want a practical guide and handbook, not a philosophical treatise. It is an instructor in the use of the universal Principle of Life, and my effort has been to explain the way in so plain and simple a fashion that the reader, though he may have given no previous study to New Thought or metaphysics, may readily follow it to perfect health. While retaining all essentials, I have carefully eliminated all non-essentials; I have used no technical, abstruse, or difficult language, and have kept the one point in view at all times.

As its title asserts, the book deals with science, not speculation. The monistic theory of the universe — the theory that matter, mind, consciousness, and life are all manifestations of one Substance — is now accepted by most thinkers; and if you accept this theory, you cannot deny the logical conclusions you will find herein. Best of all, the methods of thought and action prescribed have been tested by the author in his own case, and in the case of hundreds of others during twelve years of practice, with continuous and unfailing success. I can say of the Science of Being Well that it works; and that wherever its laws are complied with, it can no more fail to work than the science of geometry can fail to work. If the tissues of your body have not been so destroyed that continued life is impossible, you can get well; and if you will think and act in a Certain Way, you will get well.

If the reader wishes to fully understand the monistic theory of the cosmos, he is recommended to read Hegel and Emerson. Those who wish more detailed information as to the performance of the voluntary functions — eating, drinking, breathing, and sleeping — may read "New Science of Living and Healing," "Letters to a Woman's Husband," and "The Constructive Use of Foods," booklets by W. D. Wattles. I would also recommend the writings of Horace Fletcher, and of Edward Hooker Dewey. Read all these, if you like, as a sort of buttress to your faith; but let me warn you against making the mistake of studying many conflicting theories, and practicing, at the same time, parts of several different "systems"; for if you get well, it must be by giving your WHOLE MIND to the right way of thinking and living. Remember that the SCIENCE OF BEING WELL claims to be a complete and sufficient guide in every particular. Concentrate upon the way of thinking and acting it prescribes, and follow it in every detail, and you will get well; or if you are already well, you will remain so. I trust that you will go on until the priceless blessing of perfect health is yours.

WALLACE D. WATTLES, 1910

Chapter 1
The Principle of Health

In the personal application of the Science of Being Well, as in that of the Science of Getting Rich, certain fundamental truths must be known in the beginning, and accepted without question. Some of these truths we state here:

The perfectly natural performance of function constitutes health; and the perfectly natural performance of function results from the natural action of the Principle of Life. There is a Principle of Life in the universe; it is the One Living Substance from which all things are made. This Living Substance permeates, penetrates, and fills the interspaces of the universe; it is in and through all things, like a very refined and diffusible ether. All life comes from it; its life is all the life there is.

Man is a form of this Living Substance, and has within him a Principle of Health. (The word Principle is used as meaning source.) The Principle of Health in man, when in full constructive activity, causes all the voluntary functions of his life to be perfectly performed.

It is the Principle of Health in man which really works all healing, no matter what "system" or "remedy" is employed; and this Principle of Health is brought into Constructive Activity by thinking in a Certain Way.

I proceed now to prove this last statement. We all know that cures are wrought by all the different, and often opposite, methods employed in the various branches of the healing art. The allopath, who gives a strong dose of a counter-poison, cures his patient; and the homeopath, who gives a diminutive dose of the poison most similar to that of the disease, also cures it. If allopathy ever cured any given disease, it is certain that homeopathy never cured that disease; and if homeopathy ever cured an ailment, allopathy could not possibly cure that ailment. The two systems are radically opposite in theory and practice; and yet both "cure" most diseases. And even the remedies used by physicians in any one school are not the same. Go with a case of indigestion to half a dozen doctors, and compare their prescriptions; it is more than likely that none of the ingredients of any one of them will be in the others. Must we not conclude that their patients are healed by a Principle of Health within themselves, and not by something in the varying "remedies"?

Not only this, but we find the same ailments cured by the osteopath with manipulations of the spine; by the faith healer with prayer, by the food scientist with bills of fare, by the Christian Scientist with a formulated creed statement, by the mental scientist with affirmation, and by the hygienists with differing plans of living. What conclusion can we come to in the face of all these facts but that there is a Principle of Health which is the same in all people, and which really accomplishes all the cures; and that there is something in all the "systems" which, under favorable conditions, arouses the Principle of Health to action? That is, medicines, manipulations, prayers, bills of fare, affirmations, and hygienic practices cure whenever they cause the Principle of Health to become active; and fail whenever they do not cause it to become active. Does not all this indicate that the results depend upon the way the patient thinks about the remedy, rather than upon the ingredients in the prescription?

There is an old story which furnishes so good an illustration on this point that I will give it here. It is said that in the middle ages, the bones of a saint, kept in one of the monasteries, were working miracles of healing; on certain days a great crowd of the afflicted gathered to touch the relics, and all who did so were healed. On the eve of one of these occasions, some sacrilegious rascal gained access to the case in which the wonder-working relics were kept and stole the bones; and in the morning, with the usual crowd of sufferers waiting at the gates, the fathers found themselves shorn of the source of the miracle-working power. They resolved to keep the matter quiet, hoping that by doing so they might find the thief and recover their treasures; and hastening to the cellar of the convent they dug up the bones of a murderer, who had been buried there many years before. These they placed in the case, intending to make some plausible excuse for the failure of the saint to perform his usual miracles on that day; and then they let in the waiting assemblage of the sick and infirm. To the intense astonishment of those in the secret, the bones of the malefactor proved as efficacious as those of the saint; and the healing went on as before. One of the fathers is said to have left a history of the occurrence, in which he confessed that, in his judgment, the healing power had been in the people themselves all the time, and never in the bones at all.

Whether the story is true or not, the conclusion applies to all the cures wrought by all the systems. The Power that Heals is in the patient himself; and whether it shall become active or not does not depend upon the physical or mental means used, but upon the way the patient thinks about these means. There is a Universal Principle of Life, as Jesus taught; a great spiritual Healing Power; and there is a Principle of Health in man which is related to this Healing Power. This is dormant or active, according to the way a man thinks. He can always quicken it into activity by thinking in a Certain Way.

Your getting well does not depend upon the adoption of some system, or the finding of some remedy; people with your identical ailments have been healed by all systems and all remedies. It does not depend upon climate; some people are well and others are sick in all climates. It does not depend upon avocation, unless in case of those who work under poisonous conditions; people are well in all trades and professions. Your getting well depends upon your beginning to think — and act — in a Certain Way.

The way a man thinks about things is determined by what he believes about them. His thoughts are determined by his faith, and the results depend upon his making a personal application of his faith. If a man has faith in the efficacy of a medicine, and is able to apply that faith to himself, that medicine will certainly cause him to be cured; but though his faith be great, he will not be cured unless he applies it to himself. Many sick people have faith for others but none for themselves. So, if he has faith in a system of diet, and can personally apply that faith, it will cure him; and if he has faith in prayers and affirmations and personally applies his faith, prayers and affirmations will cure him. Faith, personally applied, cures; and no matter how great the faith or how persistent the thought, it will not cure without personal application. The Science of Being Well, then, includes the two fields of thought and action. To be well it is not enough that man should merely think in a Certain Way; he must apply his thought to himself, and he must express and externalize it in his outward life by acting in the same way that he thinks.

Chapter 2
The Foundations of Faith

Before man can think in the Certain Way which will cause his diseases to be healed, he must believe in certain truths which are here stated:

All things are made from one Living Substance, which, in its original state, permeates, penetrates, and fills the interspaces of the universe. While all visible things are made from It, yet this Substance, in its first formless condition is in and through all the visible forms that It has made. Its life is in All, and its intelligence is in All.

This Substance creates by thought, and its method is by taking the form of that which it thinks about. The thought of a form held by this substance causes it to assume that form; the thought of a motion causes it to institute that motion. Forms are created by this substance in moving itself into certain attitudes or positions. When Original Substance wishes to create a given form, it thinks of the motions which will produce that form. When it wishes to create a world, it thinks of the motions, perhaps extending through ages, which will result in its coming into the attitude and form of the world; and these motions are made. When it wishes to create an oak tree, it thinks of the sequences of movement, perhaps extending through ages, which will result in the form of an oak tree; and these motions are made. The particular sequences of motion by which differing forms should be produced were established in the beginning; they are changeless. Certain motions instituted in the Formless Substance will forever produce certain forms.

Man's body is formed from the Original Substance, and is the result of certain motions, which first existed as thoughts of Original Substance. The motions which produce, renew, and repair the body of man are called functions, and these functions are of two classes: voluntary and involuntary. The involuntary functions are under the control of the Principle of Health in man, and are performed in a perfectly healthy manner so long as man thinks in a certain way. The voluntary functions of life are eating, drinking, breathing, and sleeping. These, entirely or in part, are under the direction of man's conscious mind; and he can perform them in a perfectly healthy way if he will. If he does not perform them in a healthy way, he cannot long be well. So we see that if man thinks in a certain way, and eats, drinks, breathes, and sleeps in a corresponding way, he will be well.

The involuntary functions of man's life are under the direct control of the Principle of Health, and so long as man thinks in a perfectly healthy way, these functions are perfectly performed; for the action of the Principle of Health is largely directed by man's conscious thought, affecting his sub-conscious mind.

Man is a thinking center, capable of originating thought; and as he does not know everything, he makes mistakes and thinks error. Not knowing everything, he believes things to be true which are not true. Man holds in his thought the idea of diseased and abnormal functioning and conditions, and so perverts the action of the Principle of Health, causing diseased and abnormal functioning and conditions within his own body. In the Original Substance there are held only the thoughts of perfect motion; perfect and healthy function; complete life. God never thinks disease or imperfection. But for countless ages men have held thoughts of disease, abnormality, old age, and death; and the perverted functioning resulting from these thoughts has become a part of the inheritance of the race. Our ancestors have, for many generations, held imperfect ideas concerning human form and functioning; and we begin life with racial sub-conscious impressions of imperfection and disease.

This is not natural, or a part of the plan of nature. The purpose of nature can be nothing else than the perfection of life. This we see from the very nature of life itself. It is the nature of life to continually advance toward more perfect living; advancement is the inevitable result of the very act of living. Increase is always the result of active living; whatever lives must live more and more. The seed, lying in the granary, has life, but it is not living. Put it into the soil and it becomes active, and at once begins to gather to itself from the surrounding substance, and to build a plant form. It will so cause increase that a seed head will be produced containing thirty, sixty, or a hundred seeds, each having as much life as the first.

Life, by living, increases.

Life cannot live without increasing, and the fundamental impulse of life is to live. It is in response to this fundamental impulse that Original Substance works, and creates. God must live; and he cannot live except as he creates and increases. In multiplying forms, He is moving on to live more.

The universe is a Great Advancing Life, and the purpose of nature is the advancement of life toward perfection; toward perfect functioning. The purpose of nature is perfect health.

The purpose of Nature, so far as man is concerned, is that he should be continuously advancing into more life, and progressing toward perfect life; and that he should live the most complete life possible in his present sphere of action.

This must be so, because That which lives in man is seeking more life.

Give a little child a pencil and paper, and he begins to draw crude figures; That which lives in him is trying to express Itself in art. Give him a set of blocks, and he will try to build something; That which lives in him is seeking expression

The Science of Being Well

in architecture. Seat him at a piano, and he will try to draw harmony from the keys; That which lives in him is trying to express Itself in music. That which lives in man is always seeking to live more; and since man lives most when he is well, the Principle of Nature in him can seek only health. The natural state of man is a state of perfect health; and everything in him, and in nature, tends toward health.

Sickness can have no place in the thought of Original Substance, for it is by its own nature continually impelled toward the fullest and most perfect life; therefore, toward health. Man, as he exists in the thought of the Formless Substance, has perfect health. Disease, which is abnormal or perverted function — motion imperfectly made, or made in the direction of imperfect life — has no place in the thought of the Thinking Stuff.

The Supreme Mind never thinks of disease. Disease was not created or ordained by God, or sent forth from him. It is wholly a product of separate consciousness; of the individual thought of man. God, the Formless Substance, does not see disease, think disease, know disease, or recognize disease. Disease is recognized only by the thought of man; God thinks nothing but health.

From all the foregoing, we see that health is a fact or TRUTH in the original substance from which we are all formed; and that disease is imperfect functioning, resulting from the imperfect thoughts of men, past and present. If man's thoughts of himself had always been those of perfect health, man could not possibly now be otherwise than perfectly healthy.

Man in perfect health is the thought of Original Substance, and man in imperfect health is the result of his own failure to think perfect health, and to perform the voluntary functions of life in a healthy way. We will here arrange in a syllabus the basic truths of the Science of Being Well:

- There is a Thinking Substance from which all things are made, and which, in its original state, permeates, penetrates, and fills the interspaces of the universe. It is the life of All.
- The thought of a form in this Substance causes the form; the thought of a motion produces the motion. In relation to man, the thoughts of this Substance are always of perfect functioning and perfect health.
- Man is a thinking center, capable of original thought; and his thought has power over his own functioning. By thinking imperfect thoughts he has caused imperfect and perverted functioning; and by performing the voluntary functions of life in a perverted manner, he has assisted in causing disease.
- If man will think only thoughts of perfect health, he can cause within himself the functioning of perfect health; all the Power of Life will be exerted to assist him. But this healthy functioning will not

continue unless man performs the external, or voluntary, functions of living in a healthy manner.
- Man's first step must be to learn how to think perfect health; and his second step to learn how to eat, drink, breathe, and sleep in a perfectly healthy way. If man takes these two steps, he will certainly become well, and remain so.

Chapter 3
Life and Its Organisms

The human body is the abiding place of an energy which renews it when worn; which eliminates waste or poisonous matter, and which repairs the body when broken or injured. This energy we call life. Life is not generated or produced within the body; it produces the body.

The seed which has been kept in the storehouse for years will grow when planted in the soil; it will produce a plant. But the life in the plant is not generated by its growing; it is the life which makes the plant grow.

The performance of function does not cause life; it is life which causes function to be performed. Life is first; function afterward.

It is life which distinguishes organic from inorganic matter, but it is not produced after the organization of matter.

Life is the principle or force which causes organization; it builds organisms. It is a principle or force inherent in Original Substance; all life is One.

This Life Principle of the All is the Principle of Health in man, and becomes constructively active whenever man thinks in a certain way. Whoever, therefore, thinks in this Certain Way will surely have perfect health if his external functioning is in conformity with his thought. But the external functioning must conform to the thought; man cannot hope to be well by thinking health, if he eats, drinks, breathes, and sleeps like a sick man.

The universal Life Principle, then, is the Principle of Health in man. It is one with original substance. There is one Original Substance from which all things are made; this substance is alive, and its life is the Principle of Life of the universe. This Substance has created from itself all the forms of organic life by thinking them, or by thinking the motions and functions which produce them.

Original Substance thinks only health, because It knows all truth; there is no truth which is not known in the Formless, which is All, and in all. It not only knows all truth, but it has all power; its vital power is the source of all the energy there is. A conscious life which knows all truth and which has all power cannot go wrong or perform function imperfectly; knowing all, it knows, too much to go wrong, and so the Formless cannot be diseased or think disease.

Man is a form of this original substance, and has a separate consciousness of his own; but his consciousness is limited, and therefore imperfect. By reason of his limited knowledge man can and does think wrongly, and so he causes perverted and imperfect functioning in his own body. Man has not known too much to go wrong. The diseased or imperfect functioning may not instantly result from an imperfect thought, but it is bound to come if the thought becomes habitual. Any thought continuously held by man tends to the establishment of the corresponding condition in his body.

Also, man has failed to learn how to perform the voluntary functions of his life in a healthy way. He does not know when, what, and how to eat; he knows little about breathing, and less about sleep. He does all these things in a wrong way, and under wrong conditions; and this because he has neglected to follow the only sure guide to the knowledge of life. He has tried to live by logic rather than by instinct; he has made living a matter of art, and not of nature. And he has gone wrong.

His only remedy is to begin to go right; and this he can surely do. It is the work of this book to teach the whole truth, so that the man who reads it shall know too much to go wrong.

The thoughts of disease produce the forms of disease. Man must learn to think health; and being Original Substance which takes the form of its thoughts, he will become the form of health and manifest perfect health in all his functioning. The people who were healed by touching the bones of the saint were really healed by thinking in a certain way, and not by any power emanating from the relics. There is no healing power in the bones of dead men, whether they be those of saint or sinner.

The people who were healed by the doses of either the allopath or the homeopath were also really healed by thinking in a certain way; there is no drug which has within itself the power to heal disease.

The people who have been healed by prayers and affirmations were also healed by thinking in a certain way; there is no curative power in strings of words.

All the sick who have been healed, by whatsoever "system," have thought in a certain way; and a little examination will show us what this way is.

The two essentials of the Way are Faith, and a Personal Application of the Faith.

The people who touched the saint's bones had faith; and so great was their faith that in the instant they touched the relics they SEVERED ALL MENTAL RELATIONS WITH DISEASE, AND MENTALLY UNIFIED THEMSELVES WITH HEALTH.

This change of mind was accompanied by an intense devotional FEELING which penetrated to the deepest recesses of their souls, and so aroused the Principle of Health to powerful action. By faith they claimed that they were healed, or appropriated health to themselves; and in full faith they ceased to think of themselves in connection with disease and thought of themselves only in connection with health.

These are the two essentials to thinking in the Certain Way which will make you well: first, claim or appropriate health by faith; and, second, sever all mental relations with disease, and enter into mental relations with health. That which we make ourselves, mentally, we become physically; and that with which we unite ourselves mentally we become unified with physically. If your thought always relates you to disease, then your thought becomes a fixed power to cause disease within you; and if your thought always relates you to health, then your thought becomes a fixed power exerted to keep you well.

In the case of the people who are healed by medicines, the result is obtained in the same way. They have, consciously or unconsciously, sufficient faith in the means used to cause them to sever mental relations with disease and enter into mental relations with health. Faith may be unconscious. It is possible for us to have a sub-conscious or inbred faith in things like medicine, in which we do not believe to any extent objectively; and this sub-conscious faith may be quite sufficient to quicken the Principle of Health into constructive activity. Many who have little conscious faith are healed in this way; while many others who have great faith in the means are not healed because they do not make the personal application to themselves; their faith is general, but not specific for their own cases.

In the Science of Being Well we have two main points to consider: first, how to think with faith; and, second, how to so apply the thought to ourselves as to quicken the Principle of Health into constructive activity. We begin by learning What to Think.

Chapter 4
What to Think

In order to sever all mental relations with disease, you must enter into mental relations with health, making the process positive, not negative; one of assumption, not of rejection. You are to receive or appropriate health rather than to reject and deny disease. Denying disease accomplishes next to nothing; it does little good to cast out the devil and leave the house vacant, for he will presently return with others worse than himself. When you enter into full and constant mental relations with health, you must of necessity cease all relationship with disease. The first step in the Science of Being Well is, then, to enter into complete thought connection with health.

The best way to do this is to form a mental image or picture of yourself as being well, imagining a perfectly strong and healthy body; and to spend sufficient time in contemplating this image to make it your habitual thought of yourself.

This is not so easy as it sounds; it necessitates the taking of considerable time for meditation, and not all persons have the imaging faculty well enough developed to form a distinct mental picture of themselves in a perfect or idealized body. It is much easier, as in "The Science of Getting Rich," to form a mental image of the things one wants to have; for we have seen these things, or their counterparts, and know how they look; we can picture them very easily from memory. But we have never seen ourselves in a perfect body, and a clear mental image is hard to form.

It is not necessary or essential, however, to have a clear mental image of yourself as you wish to be; it is only essential to form a CONCEPTION of perfect health, and to relate yourself to it. This Conception of Health is not a mental picture of a particular thing; it is an understanding of health, and carries with it the idea of perfect functioning in every part and organ.

You may TRY to picture yourself as perfect in physique; that helps; and you MUST think of yourself as doing everything in the manner of a perfectly strong and healthy person. You can picture yourself as walking down the street with an erect body and a vigorous stride; you can picture yourself as doing your day's work easily and with surplus vigor, never tired or weak; you can picture in your mind how all things would be done by a person full of health and power, and you can make yourself the central figure in the picture, doing things in just that way. Never think of the ways in which weak or sickly people do things; always think of the way strong people do things. Spend your leisure time in thinking about the Strong Way, until you have a good conception of it; and always think of yourself in connection with the Strong Way of Doing Things. That is what I mean by having a Conception of Health.

In order to establish perfect functioning in every part, man does not have to study anatomy or physiology, so that he can form a mental image of each separate organ and address himself to it. He does not have to "treat" his liver, his kidneys, his stomach, or his heart. There is one Principle of Health in man, which has control over all the involuntary functions of his life; and the thought of perfect health, impressed upon this Principle, will reach each part and organ. Man's liver is not controlled by a liver-principle, his stomach by a digestive principle, and so on; the Principle of Health is One.

The less you go into the detailed study of physiology, the better for you. Our knowledge of this science is very imperfect, and leads to imperfect thought. Imperfect thought causes imperfect functioning, which is disease. Let me illustrate: Until quite recently, physiology fixed ten days as the extreme limit of man's endurance without food; it was considered that only in exceptional cases could he survive a longer fast. So the impression became universally disseminated that one who was deprived of food must die in from five to ten days; and numbers of people, when cut off from food by shipwreck, accident, or famine, did die within this period. But the performances of Dr. Tanner, the forty-day faster, and the writings of Dr. Dewey and others on the fasting cure, together with the experiments of numberless people who have fasted from forty to sixty days, have shown that man's ability to live without food is vastly greater than had been supposed. Any person, properly educated, can fast from twenty to forty days with little loss in weight, and often with no apparent loss of strength at all. The people who starved to death in ten days or less did so because they believed that death was inevitable; an erroneous physiology had given them a wrong thought about themselves. When a man is deprived of food he will die in from ten to fifty days, according to the way he has been taught; or, in other words, according to the way he thinks about it. So you see that an erroneous physiology can work very mischievous results.

No Science of Being Well can be founded on current physiology; it is not sufficiently exact in its knowledge. With all its pretensions, comparatively little is really known as to the interior workings and processes of the body. It is not known just how food is digested; it is not known just what part food plays, if any, in the generation of force. It is not known exactly what the liver, spleen, and pancreas are for, or what part their secretions play in the chemistry of assimilation. On all these and most other points we theorize, but we do not really know. When man begins to study physiology, he enters the domain of theory and disputation; he comes among conflicting opinions, and he is bound to form mistaken ideas concerning himself. These mistaken ideas lead to the thinking of wrong thoughts, and this leads to perverted functioning and disease. All that the most perfect knowledge of physiology could do for man would be to enable him to think only thoughts of perfect health, and to eat, drink, breathe, and sleep in a perfectly healthy way; and this, as we shall show, he can do without studying physiology at all.

This, for the most part, is true of all hygiene. There are certain fundamental propositions which we should know; and these will be explained in later chapters, but aside from these propositions, ignore physiology and hygiene. They tend to fill your mind with thoughts of imperfect conditions, and these thoughts will produce the imperfect conditions in your own body. You cannot study any "science" which recognizes disease, if you are to think nothing but health.

Drop all investigation as to your present condition, its causes, or possible results, and set yourself to the work of forming a conception of health.

Think about health and the possibilities of health; of the work that may be done and the pleasures that may be enjoyed in a condition of perfect health. Then make this conception your guide in thinking of yourself; refuse to entertain for an instant any thought of yourself which is not in harmony with it. When any idea of disease or imperfect functioning enters your mind, cast it out instantly by calling up a thought which is in harmony with the Conception of Health.

Think of yourself at all times as realizing conception; as being a strong and perfectly healthy personage; and do not harbor a contrary thought.

KNOW that as you think of yourself in unity with this conception, the Original Substance which permeates and fills the tissues of your body is taking form according to the thought; and know that this Intelligent Substance or mind stuff will cause function to be performed in such a way that your body will be rebuilt with perfectly healthy cells.

The Intelligent Substance, from which all things are made, permeates and penetrates all things; and so it is in and through your body. It moves according to its thoughts; and so if you hold only the thoughts of perfectly healthy function, it will cause the movements of perfectly healthy function within you.

Hold with persistence to the thought of perfect health in relation to yourself; do not permit yourself to think in any other way. Hold this thought with perfect faith that it is the fact, the truth. It is the truth so far as your mental body is concerned. You have a mind-body and a physical body; the mind-body takes form just as you think of yourself, and any thought which you hold continuously is made visible by the transformation of the physical body into its image. Implanting the thought of perfect functioning in the mind-body will, in due time, cause perfect functioning in the physical body.

The transformation of the physical body into the image of the ideal held by the mind-body is not accomplished instantaneously; we cannot transfigure

The Science of Being Well

our physical bodies at will as Jesus did. In the creation and recreation of forms, Substance moves along the fixed lines of growth it has established; and the impression upon it of the health thought causes the healthy body to be built cell by cell. Holding only thoughts of perfect health will ultimately cause perfect functioning; and perfect functioning will in due time produce a perfectly healthy body. It may be as well to condense this chapter into a syllabus:

- Your physical body is permeated and fitted with an Intelligent Substance, which forms a body of mind-stuff. This mind-stuff controls the functioning of your physical body. A thought of disease or of imperfect function, impressed upon the mind-stuff, causes disease or imperfect functioning in the physical body. If you are diseased, it is because wrong thoughts have made impressions on this mind-stuff; these may have been either your own thoughts or those of your parents; we begin life with many sub-conscious impressions, both right and wrong. But the natural tendency of all mind is toward health, and if no thoughts are held in the conscious mind save those of health, all internal functioning will come to be performed in a perfectly healthy manner.

- The Power of Nature within you is sufficient to overcome all hereditary impressions, and if you will learn to control your thoughts, so that you shall think only those of health, and if you will perform the voluntary functions of life in a perfectly healthy way, you can certainly be well.

Chapter 5
Faith

The Principle of Health is moved by Faith; nothing else can call it into action, and only faith can enable you to relate yourself to health, and sever your relation with disease, in your thoughts.

You will continue to think of disease unless you have faith in health. If you do not have faith you will doubt; if you doubt, you will fear; and if you fear, you will relate yourself in mind to that which you fear.

If you fear disease, you will think of yourself in connection with disease; and that will produce within yourself the form and motions of disease. Just as Original Substance creates from itself the forms of its thoughts, so your mind-body, which is original substance, takes the form and motion of whatever you think about. If you fear disease, dread disease, have doubts about your safety from disease, or if you even contemplate disease, you will connect yourself with it and create its forms and motions within you.

Let me enlarge somewhat upon this point. The potency, or creative power, of a thought is given to it by the faith that is in it.

Thoughts which contain no faith create no forms.

The Formless Substance, which knows all truth and therefore thinks only truth, has perfect faith in every thought, because it thinks only truth; and so all its thoughts create.

But if you will imagine a thought in Formless Substance in which there was no faith, you will see that such a thought could not cause the Substance to move or take form.

Keep in mind the fact that only those thoughts which are conceived in faith have creative energy. Only those thoughts which have faith with them are able to change function, or to quicken the Principle of Health into activity.

If you do not have faith in health, you will certainly have faith in disease. If you do not have faith in health, it will do you no good to think about health, for your thoughts will have no potency, and will cause no change for the better in your conditions. If you do not have faith in health, I repeat, you will have faith in disease; and if, under such conditions, you think about health for ten hours a day, and think about disease for only a few minutes, the disease thought will control your condition because it will have the potency of faith, while the health thought will not. Your mind-body will take on the form and motions of disease and retain them, because your health thought will not have sufficient dynamic force to change form or motion.

In order to practice the Science of Being Well, you must have complete faith in health.

Faith begins in belief; and we now come to the question: What must you believe in order to have faith in health?

You must believe that there is more health-power than disease-power in both yourself and your environment; and you cannot help believing this if you consider the facts. These are the facts:

- There is a Thinking Substance from which all things are made, and which, in its original state, permeates, penetrates, and fills the interspaces of the universe.
- The thought of a form, in this Substance, produces the form; the thought of a motion institutes the motion. In relation to man, the thoughts of Original Substance are always of perfect health and perfect functioning. This Substance, within and without man, always exerts its power toward health.
- Man is a thinking center, capable of original thought. He has a mind-body of Original Substance permeating a physical body; and the functioning of his physical body is determined by the FAITH of his mind-body. If man thinks with faith of the functioning of health, he will cause his internal functions to be performed in a healthy manner, provided that he performs the external functions in a corresponding manner. But if man thinks, with faith, of disease, or of the power of disease, he will cause his internal functioning to be the functioning of disease.
- The Original Intelligent Substance is in man, moving toward health; and it is pressing upon him from every side. Man lives, moves, and has his being in a limitless ocean of health-power; and he uses this power according to his faith. If he appropriates it and applies it to himself it is all his; and if he unifies himself with it by unquestioning faith, he cannot fail to attain health, for the power of this Substance is all the power there is.

A belief in the above statements is a foundation for faith in health. If you believe them, you believe that health is the natural state of man, and that man lives in the midst of Universal Health; that all the power of nature makes for health, and that health is possible to all, and can surely be attained by all. You will believe that the power of health in the universe is ten thousand times greater than that of disease; in fact, that disease has no power whatever, being only the result of perverted thought and faith. And if you believe that health is possible to you, and that it may surely be attained by you, and that you know exactly what to do in order to attain it, you will have faith in health. You will have this faith and knowledge if you read this book through with care and determine to believe in and practice its teachings.

It is not merely the possession of faith, but the personal application of faith which works healing. You must claim health in the beginning, and form a conception of health, and, as far as may be, of yourself as a perfectly healthy person; and then, by faith, you must claim that you ARE REALIZING this conception.

Do not assert with faith that you are going to get well; assert with faith that you ARE well.

Having faith in health, and applying it to yourself, means having faith that you are healthy; and the first step in this is to claim that it is the truth.

Mentally take the attitude of being well, and do not say anything or do anything which contradicts this attitude. Never speak a word or assume a physical attitude which does not harmonize with the claim: "I am perfectly well." When you walk, go with a brisk step, and with your chest thrown out and your head held up; watch that at all times your physical actions and attitudes are those of a healthy person. When you find that you have relapsed into the attitude of weakness or disease, change instantly; straighten up; think of health and power. Refuse to consider yourself as other than a perfectly healthy person.

One great aid — perhaps the greatest aid — in applying your faith you will find in the exercise of gratitude.

Whenever you think of yourself, or of your advancing condition, give thanks to the Great Intelligent Substance for the perfect health you are enjoying.

Remember that, as Swedenborg taught, there is a continual inflow of life from the Supreme, which is received by all created things according to their forms; and by man according to his faith. Health from God is continually being urged upon you; and when you think of this, lift up your mind reverently to Him, and give thanks that you have been led to the Truth and into perfect health of mind and body. Be, all the time, in a grateful frame of mind, and let gratitude be evident in your speech.

Gratitude will help you to own and control your own field of thought.

Whenever the thought of disease is presented to you, instantly claim health, and thank God for the perfect health you have. Do this so that there shall be no room in your mind for a thought of ill. Every thought connected in any way with ill health is unwelcome, and you can close the door of your mind in its face by asserting that you are well, and by reverently thanking God that it is so. Soon the old thoughts will return no more.

Gratitude has a twofold effect; it strengthens your own faith, and it brings you into close and harmonious relations with the Supreme. You believe that there is one Intelligent Substance from which all life and all power come; you believe that you receive your own life from this substance; and you relate yourself closely to It by feeling continuous gratitude. It is easy to see that the more closely you relate yourself to the Source of Life the more readily you may receive life from it; and it is easy also to see that your relation to It is a matter of mental attitude. We cannot come into physical relationship with God, for God is mind-stuff and we also are mind-stuff; our relation with Him must therefore be a mind relation. It is plain, then, that the man who feels deep and hearty gratitude will live in closer touch with God than the man who never looks up to Him in thankfulness. The ungrateful or unthankful mind really denies that it receives at all, and so cuts its connection with the Supreme. The grateful mind is always looking toward the Supreme, and is always open to receive from it; and it will receive continually.

The Principle of Health in man receives its vital power from the Principle of Life in the universe; and man relates himself to the Principle of Life by faith in health, and by gratitude for the health he receives.

Man may cultivate both faith and gratitude by the proper use of his will.

Chapter 6
Use of the Will

In the practice of the Science of Being Well the will is not used to compel yourself to go when you are not really able to go, or to do things when you are not physically strong enough to do them. You do not direct your will upon your physical body or try to compel the proper performance of internal function by will power.

You direct the will upon the mind, and use it in determining what you shall believe, what you shall think, and to what you shall give your attention.

The will should never be used upon any person or thing external to you, and it should never be used upon your own body. The sole legitimate use of the will is in determining to what you shall give your attention, and what you shall think about the things to which your attention is given.

All belief begins in the will to believe.

You cannot always and instantly believe what you will to believe; but you can always will to believe what you want to believe. You want to believe truth about health, and you can will to do so. The statements you have been reading in this book are the truth about health, and you can will to believe them; this must be your first step toward getting well.

These are the statements you must will to believe:

- That there is a Thinking Substance from which all things are made, and that man receives the Principle of Health, which is his life, from this Substance.
- That man himself is Thinking Substance; a mind-body, permeating a physical body, and that as man's thoughts are, so will the functioning of his physical body be.
- That if man will think only thoughts of perfect health, he must and will cause the internal and involuntary functioning of his body to be the functioning of health, provided that his external and voluntary functioning and attitude are in accordance with his thoughts.

When you will to believe these statements, you must also begin to act upon them. You cannot long retain a belief unless you act upon it; you cannot increase a belief until it becomes faith unless you act upon it; and you certainly cannot expect to reap benefits in any way from a belief so long as you act as if the opposite were true. You cannot long have faith in health if you continue to act like a sick person. If you continue to act like a sick person, you cannot help continuing to think of yourself as a sick person; and if you continue to think of yourself as a sick person, you will continue to be a sick person.

The Science of Being Well

The first step toward acting externally like a well person is to begin to act internally like a well person. Form your conception of perfect health, and get into the way of thinking about perfect health until it begins to have a definite meaning to you. Picture yourself as doing the things a strong and healthy person would do, and have faith that you can and will do those things in that way; continue this until you have a vivid CONCEPTION of health, and what it means to you. When I speak in this book of a conception of health, I mean a conception that carries with it the idea of the way a healthy person looks and does things. Think of yourself in connection with health until you form a conception of how you would live, appear, act, and do things as a perfectly healthy person. Think about yourself in connection with health until you conceive of yourself, in imagination, as always doing everything in the manner of a well person; until the thought of health conveys the idea of what health means to you. As I have said in a former chapter, you may not be able to form a clear mental image of yourself in perfect health, but you can form a conception of yourself as acting like a healthy person.

Form this conception, and then think only thoughts of perfect health in relation to yourself, and, so far as may be possible, in relation to others. When a thought of sickness or disease is presented to you, reject it; do not let it get into your mind; do not entertain or consider it at all. Meet it by thinking health; by thinking that you are well, and by being sincerely grateful for the health you are receiving. Whenever suggestions of disease are coming thick and fast upon you, and you are in a "tight place," fall back upon the exercise of gratitude. Connect yourself with the Supreme; give thanks to God for the perfect health He gives you, and you will soon find yourself able to control your thoughts, and to think what you want to think. In times of doubt, trial, and temptation, the exercise of gratitude is always a sheet anchor which will prevent you from being swept away. Remember that the great essential thing is to SEVER ALL MENTAL RELATIONS WITH DISEASE, AND TO ENTER INTO FULL MENTAL RELATIONSHIP WITH HEALTH. This is the KEY to all mental healing; it is the whole thing. Here we see the secret of the great success of Christian Science; more than any other formulated system of practice, it insists that its converts shall sever relations with disease, and relate themselves fully with health. The healing power of Christian Science is not in its theological formulæ, nor in its denial of matter; but in the fact that it induces the sick to ignore disease as an unreal thing and accept health by faith as a reality. Its failures are made because its practitioners, while thinking in the Certain Way, do not eat, drink, breathe, and sleep in the same way.

While there is no healing power in the repetition of strings of words, yet it is a very convenient thing to have the central thoughts so formulated that you can repeat them readily, so that you can use them as affirmations whenever you are surrounded by an environment which gives you adverse suggestions. When those around you begin to talk of sickness and death, close your ears and mentally assert something like the following:

- There is One Substance, and I am that Substance.
- That Substance is eternal, and it is Life; I am that Substance, and I am Eternal Life.
- That Substance knows no disease; I am that Substance, and I am Health.

Exercise your will power in choosing only those thoughts which are thoughts of health, and arrange your environment so that it shall suggest thoughts of health. Do not have about you books, pictures, or other things which suggest death, disease, deformity, weakness, or age; have only those which convey the ideas of health, power, joy, vitality, and youth. When you are confronted with a book, or anything else which suggests disease, do not give it your attention. Think of your conception of health, and your gratitude, and affirm as above; use your will power to fix your attention upon thoughts of health. In a future chapter I shall touch upon this point again; what I wish to make plain here is that you must think only health, recognize only health, and give your attention only to health; and that you must control thought, recognition, and attention by the use of your will.

Do not try to use your will to compel the healthy performance of function within you. The Principle of Health will attend to that, if you give your attention only to thoughts of health.

Do not try to exert your will upon the Formless to compel It to give you more vitality or power; it is already placing all the power there is at your service.

You do not have to use your will to conquer adverse conditions, or to subdue unfriendly forces; there are no unfriendly forces; there is only One Force, and that force is friendly to you; it is a force which makes for health.

Everything in the universe wants you to be well; you have absolutely nothing to overcome but your own habit of thinking in a certain way about disease, and you can do this only by forming a habit of thinking in another Certain Way about health.

Man can cause all the internal functions of his body to be performed in a perfectly healthy manner by continuously thinking in a Certain Way, and by performing the external functions in a certain way.

He can think in this Certain Way by controlling his attention, and he can control his attention by the use of his will.

He can decide what things he will think about.

Chapter 7
Health from God

I will give a chapter here to explaining how man may receive health from the Supreme. By the Supreme I mean the Thinking Substance from which all things are made, and which is in all and through all, seeking more complete expression and fuller life. This Intelligent Substance, in a perfectly fluid state, permeates and penetrates all things, and is in touch with all minds. It is the source of all energy and power, and constitutes the "inflow" of life which Swedenborg saw, vitalizing all things. It is working to one definite end, and for the fulfillment of one purpose; and that purpose is the advancement of life toward the complete expression of Mind. When man harmonizes himself with this Intelligence, it can and will give him health and wisdom. When man holds steadily to the purpose to live more abundantly, he comes into harmony with this Supreme Intelligence.

The purpose of the Supreme Intelligence is the most Abundant Life for all; the purpose of this Supreme Intelligence for you is that you should live more abundantly. If, then, your own purpose is to live more abundantly, you are unified with the Supreme; you are working with It, and it must work with you. But as the Supreme Intelligence is in all, if you harmonize with it you must harmonize with all; and you must desire more abundant life for all as well as for yourself. Two great benefits come to you from being in harmony with the Supreme Intelligence.

First, you will receive wisdom. By wisdom I do not mean knowledge of facts so much as ability to perceive and understand facts, and to judge soundly and act rightly in all matters relating to life. Wisdom is the power to perceive truth, and the ability to make the best use of the knowledge of truth. It is the power to perceive at once the best end to aim at, and the means best adapted to attain that end. With wisdom comes poise, and the power to think rightly; to control and guide your thoughts, and to avoid the difficulties which come from wrong thinking. With wisdom you will be able to select the right courses for your particular needs, and to so govern yourself in all ways as to secure the best results. You will know how to do what you want to do. You can readily see that wisdom must be an essential attribute of the Supreme Intelligence, since That which knows all truth must be wise; and you can also see that just in proportion as you harmonize and unify your mind with that Intelligence you will have wisdom.

But I repeat that since this Intelligence is All, and in all, you can enter into Its wisdom only by harmonizing with all. If there is anything in your desires or your purpose which will bring oppression to any, or work injustice to, or cause lack of life for any, you cannot receive wisdom from the Supreme. Furthermore, your purpose for your own self must be the best.

Man can live in three general ways: for the gratification of his body, for that of his intellect, or for that of his soul. The first is accomplished by satisfying the desires for food, drink, and those other things which give enjoyable physical sensations. The second is accomplished by doing those things which cause pleasant mental sensations, such as gratifying the desire for knowledge or those for fine clothing, fame, power, and so on. The third is accomplished by giving way to the instincts of unselfish love and altruism. Man lives most wisely and completely when he functions most perfectly along all of these lines, without excess in any of them. The man who lives swinishly, for the body alone, is unwise and out of harmony with God; that man who lives solely for the cold enjoyments of the intellect, though he be absolutely moral, is unwise and out of harmony with God; and the man who lives wholly for the practice of altruism, and who throws himself away for others, is as unwise and as far from harmony with God as those who go to excess in other ways.

To come into full harmony with the Supreme, you must purpose to LIVE; to live to the utmost of your capabilities in body, mind, and soul. This must mean the full exercise of function in all the different ways, but without excess; for excess in one causes deficiency in the others. Behind your desire for health is your own desire for more abundant life; and behind that is the desire of the Formless Intelligence to live more fully in you. So, as you advance toward perfect health, hold steadily to the purpose to attain complete life, physical, mental, and spiritual; to advance in all ways, and in every way to live more; if you hold this purpose you will be given wisdom. "He that willeth to do the will of the Father shall KNOW," said Jesus. Wisdom is the most desirable gift that can come to man, for it makes him rightly self-governing.

But wisdom is not all you may receive from the Supreme Intelligence; you may receive physical energy, vitality, life force. The energy of the Formless Substance is unlimited, and permeates everything; you are already receiving or appropriating to yourself this energy in an automatic and instinctive way, but you can do so to a far greater degree if you set about it intelligently. The measure of a man's strength is not what God is willing to give him, but what he, himself, has the will and the intelligence to appropriate to himself. God gives you all there is; your only question is how much to take of the unlimited supply.

There is apparently no limit to the powers of men; and this is simply because man's power comes from the inexhaustible reservoir of the Supreme. The runner who has reached the stage of exhaustion, when his physical power seems entirely gone, by running on in a Certain Way may receive his "second wind"; his strength is renewed in a seemingly miraculous fashion, and he can go on indefinitely. And by continuing in the Certain Way, he may receive a third, fourth, and fifth "wind"; we do not know where the limit is, or how far it may be possible to extend it. The conditions are that the runner must have absolute faith that the strength will come; that he must think steadily of strength, and have perfect confidence that he has it, and that he must continue to run on. If he admits a doubt into his mind, he falls exhausted, and if he stops running to wait for the accession of strength, it will never come. His faith in strength, his faith that he can keep on running, his unwavering purpose to keep on running, and his action in keeping on seem to connect him to the source of energy in such a way as to bring him a new supply.

In a very similar manner, the sick person who has unquestioning faith in health, whose purpose brings him into harmony with the source, and who performs the voluntary functions of life in a certain way, will receive vital energy sufficient for all his needs, and for the healing of all his diseases. God, who seeks to live and express himself fully in man, delights to give man all that is needed for the most abundant life. Action and reaction are equal, and when you desire to live more, if you are in mental harmony with the Supreme, the forces which make for life begin to concentrate about you and upon you. The One Life begins to move toward you, and your environment becomes surcharged with it. Then, if you appropriate it by faith, it is yours. "Ye shall ask what ye will, and it shall be done unto you." Your Father giveth not his spirit by measure; he delights to give good gifts to you.

Chapter 8
Summary of the Mental Actions

Let me now summarize the mental actions and attitudes necessary to the practice of the Science of Being Well: first, you believe that there is a Thinking Substance, from which all things are made, and which, in its original state, permeates, penetrates, and fills the interspaces of the universe. This Substance is the Life of All, and is seeking to express more life in all. It is the Principle of Life of the universe, and the Principle of Health in man.

Man is a form of this Substance, and draws his vitality from it; he is a mind-body of original substance, permeating a physical body, and the thoughts of his mind-body control the functioning of his physical body. If man thinks no thoughts save those of perfect health, the functions of his physical body will be performed in a manner of perfect health.

If you would consciously relate yourself to the All-Health, your purpose must be to live fully on every plane of your being. You must want all that there is in life for body, mind, and soul; and this will bring you into harmony with all the life there is. The person who is in conscious and intelligent harmony with All will receive a continuous inflow of vital power from the Supreme Life; and this inflow is prevented by angry, selfish, or antagonistic mental attitudes. If you are against any part, you have severed relations with all; you will receive life, but only instinctively and automatically; not intelligently and purposefully. You can see that if you are mentally antagonistic to any part, you cannot be in complete harmony with the Whole; therefore, as Jesus directed, be reconciled to everybody and everything before you offer worship.

Want for everybody all that you want for yourself.

The reader is recommended to read what we have said in a former work ("The Science of Getting Rich") concerning the Competitive mind and the Creative mind. It is very doubtful whether one who has lost health can completely regain it so long as he remains in the competitive mind.

Being on the Creative or Good-Will plane in mind, the next step is to form a conception of yourself as in perfect health, and to hold no thoughts which are not in full harmony with this conception. Have FAITH that if you think only thoughts of health you will establish in your physical body the functioning of health; and use your will to determine that you will think only thoughts of health. Never think of yourself as sick, or as likely to be sick; never think of sickness in connection with yourself at all. And, as far as may be, shut out of your mind all thoughts of sickness in connection with others. Surround yourself as much as possible with the things which suggest the ideas of strength and health.

Have faith in health, and accept health as an actual present fact in your life. Claim health as a blessing bestowed upon you by the Supreme Life, and be deeply grateful at all times. Claim the blessing by faith; know that it is yours, and never admit a contrary thought to your mind.

Use your will-power to withhold your attention from every appearance of disease in yourself and others; do not study disease, think about it, nor speak of it. At all times, when the thought of disease is thrust upon you, move forward into the mental position of prayerful gratitude for your perfect health.

The mental actions necessary to being well may now be summed up in a single sentence: Form a conception of yourself in perfect health, and think only those thoughts which are in harmony with that conception.

That, with faith and gratitude, and the purpose to really live, covers all the requirements. It is not necessary to take mental exercises of any kind, except as described in Chapter 6, or to do wearying "stunts" in the way of affirmations, and so on. It is not necessary to concentrate the mind on the affected parts; it is far better not to think of any part as affected. It is not necessary to "treat" yourself by auto-suggestion, or to have others treat you in any way whatever. The power that heals is the Principle of Health within you; and to call this Principle into Constructive Action it is only necessary, having harmonized yourself with the All-Mind, to claim by FAITH the All-Health; and to hold that claim until it is physically manifested in all the functions of your body.

In order to hold this mental attitude of faith, gratitude, and health, however, your external acts must be only those of health. You cannot long hold the internal attitude of a well person if you continue to perform the external acts of a sick person. It is essential not only that your every thought should be a thought of health, but that your every act should be an act of health, performed in a healthy manner. If you will make every thought a thought of health, and every conscious act an act of health, it must infallibly follow that every internal and unconscious function shall come to be healthy; for all the power of life is being continually exerted toward health. We shall next consider how you may make every act an act of health.

Chapter 9
When to Eat

You cannot build and maintain a perfectly healthy body by mental action alone, or by the performance of the unconscious or involuntary functions alone. There are certain actions, more or less voluntary, which have a direct and immediate relation with the continuance of life itself; these are eating, drinking, breathing, and sleeping. No matter what man's thought or mental attitude may be, he cannot live unless he eats, drinks, breathes, and sleeps; and, moreover, he cannot be well if he eats, drinks, breathes, and sleeps in an unnatural or wrong manner. It is therefore vitally important that you should learn the right way to perform these voluntary functions, and I shall proceed to show you this way, beginning with the matter of eating, which is most important.

There has been a vast amount of controversy as to when to eat, what to eat, how to eat, and how much to eat; and all this controversy is unnecessary, for the Right Way is very easy to find. You have only to consider the Law which governs all attainment, whether of health, wealth, power, or happiness; and that law is that you must do what you can do now, where you are now; do every separate act in the most perfect manner possible, and put the power of faith into every action.

The processes of digestion and assimilation are under the supervision and control of an inner division of man's mentality, which is generally called the sub-conscious mind; and I shall use that term here in order to be understood. The sub-conscious mind is in charge of all the functions and processes of life; and when more food is needed by the body, it makes the fact known by causing a sensation called hunger. Whenever food is needed, and can be used, there is hunger; and whenever there is hunger it is time to eat. When there is no hunger it is unnatural and wrong to eat, no matter how great may APPEAR to be the need for food. Even if you are in a condition of apparent starvation, with great emaciation, if there is no hunger you may know that FOOD CANNOT BE USED, and it will be unnatural and wrong for you to eat. Though you have not eaten for days, weeks, or months, if you have no hunger you may be perfectly sure that food cannot be used, and will probably not be used if taken. Whenever food is needed, if there is power to digest and assimilate it, so that it can be normally used, the sub-conscious mind will announce the fact by a decided hunger. Food, taken when there is no hunger, will sometimes be digested and assimilated, because Nature makes a special effort to perform the task which is thrust upon her against her will; but if food be habitually taken when there is no hunger, the digestive power is at last destroyed, and numberless evils caused.

The Science of Being Well

If the foregoing be true — and it is indisputably so — it is a self-evident proposition that the natural time, and the healthy time, to eat is when one is hungry; and that it is never a natural or a healthy action to eat when one is not hungry. You see, then, that it is an easy matter to scientifically settle the question when to eat. ALWAYS eat when you are hungry; and NEVER eat when you are not hungry. This is obedience to nature, which is obedience to God.

We must not fail, however, to make clear the distinction between hunger and appetite. Hunger is the call of the sub-conscious mind for more material to be used in repairing and renewing the body, and in keeping up the internal heat; and hunger is never felt unless there is need for more material, and unless there is power to digest it when taken into the stomach. Appetite is a desire for the gratification of sensation. The drunkard has an appetite for liquor, but he cannot have a hunger for it. A normally fed person cannot have a hunger for candy or sweets; the desire for these things is an appetite. You cannot hunger for tea, coffee, spiced foods, or for the various taste-tempting devices of the skilled cook; if you desire these things, it is with appetite, not with hunger. Hunger is nature's call for material to be used in building new cells, and nature never calls for anything which may not be legitimately used for this purpose.

Appetite is often largely a matter of habit; if one eats or drinks at a certain hour, and especially if one takes sweetened or spiced and stimulating foods, the desire comes regularly at the same hour; but this habitual desire for food should never be mistaken for hunger. Hunger does not appear at specified times. It only comes when work or exercise has destroyed sufficient tissue to make the taking in of new raw material a necessity.

For instance, if a person has been sufficiently fed on the preceding day, it is impossible that he should feel a genuine hunger on arising from refreshing sleep. In sleep the body is recharged with vital power, and the assimilation of the food which has been taken during the day is completed; the system has no need for food immediately after sleep, unless the person went to his rest in a state of starvation. With a system of feeding, which is even a reasonable approach to a natural one, no one can have a real hunger for an early morning breakfast. There is no such thing possible as a normal or genuine hunger immediately after arising from sound sleep. The early morning breakfast is always taken to gratify appetite, never to satisfy hunger. No matter who you are, or what your condition is; no matter how hard you work, or how much you are exposed, unless you go to your bed starved, you cannot arise from your bed hungry.

Hunger is not caused by sleep, but by work. And it does not matter who you are, or what your condition, or how hard or easy your work, the so-called no-breakfast plan is the right plan for you. It is the right plan for everybody, because it is based on the universal law that hunger never comes until it is EARNED.

I am aware that a protest against this will come from the large number of people who "enjoy" their breakfasts; whose breakfast is their "best meal"; who believe that their work is so hard that they cannot "get through the forenoon on an empty stomach," and so on. But all their arguments fall down before the facts. They enjoy their breakfast as the drunkard enjoys his morning spirits, because it gratifies a habitual appetite and not because it supplies a natural want. It is their best meal for the same reason that his morning spirits are the drunkard's best drink. And they CAN get along without it, because millions of people, of every trade and profession, DO get along without it, and are vastly better for doing so. If you are to live according to the Science of Being Well, you must NEVER EAT UNTIL YOU HAVE AN EARNED HUNGER.

But if I do not eat on arising in the morning, when shall I take my first meal?

In ninety-nine cases out of a hundred twelve o'clock, noon, is early enough; and it is generally the most convenient time. If you are doing heavy work, you will get by noon a hunger sufficient to justify a good-sized meal; and if your work is light, you will probably still have hunger enough for a moderate meal. The best general rule or law that can be laid down is that you should eat your first meal of the day at noon, if you are hungry; and if you are not hungry, wait until you become so.

And when shall I eat my second meal?

Not at all, unless you are hungry for it; and that with a genuine earned hunger. If you do get hungry for a second meal, eat at the most convenient time; but do not eat until you have a really earned hunger. The reader who wishes to fully inform himself as to the reasons for this way of arranging the mealtimes will find the best books thereon cited in the preface to this work. From the foregoing, however, you can easily see that the Science of Being Well readily answers the question: When, and how often shall I eat? The answer is: Eat when you have an earned hunger; and never eat at any other time.

Chapter 10
What to Eat

The current sciences of medicine and hygiene have made no progress toward answering the question, What shall I eat? The contests between the vegetarians and the meat eaters, the cooked food advocates, raw food advocates, and various other "schools" of theorists, seem to be interminable; and from the mountains of evidence and argument piled up for and against each special theory, it is plain that if we depend on these scientists we shall never know what is the natural food of man. Turning away from the whole controversy, then, we will ask the question of nature herself, and we shall find that she has not left us without an answer.

Most of the errors of dietary scientists grow out of a false premise as to the natural state of man. It is assumed that civilization and mental development are unnatural things; that the man who lives in a modern house, in city or country, and who works in modern trade or industry for his living is leading an unnatural life, and is in an unnatural environment; that the only "natural" man is a naked savage, and that the farther we get from the savage the farther we are from nature. This is wrong. The man who has all that art and science can give him is leading the most natural life, because he is living most completely in all his faculties. The dweller in a well-appointed city flat, with modern conveniences and good ventilation, is living a far more naturally human life than the savage who lives in a hollow tree or a hole in the ground.

That Great Intelligence, which is in all and through all, has in reality practically settled the question as to what we shall eat. In ordering the affairs of nature, It has decided that man's food shall be according to the zone in which he lives. In the frigid regions of the far North, fuel foods are required. The Esquimaux live largely on the blubber and fat of aquatic animals. No other diet is possible to them; they could not get fruits, nuts, or vegetables even if they were disposed to eat them; and they could not live on them in that climate if they could get them. So, notwithstanding the arguments of the vegetarians, the Esquimaux will continue to live on animal fats.

On the other hand, as we come toward the tropics, we find fuel foods less required; and we find the people naturally inclining toward a vegetarian diet. Millions live on rice and fruits; and the food regimen of an Esquimaux village, if followed upon the equator, would result in speedy death. A "natural" diet for the equatorial regions would be very far from being a natural diet near the North Pole; and the people of either zone, if not interfered with by medical or dietary "scientists," will be guided by the All Intelligence, which seeks the fullest life in all, to feed themselves in the best way for the promotion of perfect health. In general, you can see that God, working in nature and in the evolution of human society and customs, has answered your question as to what you shall eat; and I advise you to take His answer in preference to that of any man.

In the temperate zone we find the greatest variety of foods provided by nature. And it is really quite useless and superfluous to theorize on the question what the masses shall eat, for they have no choice; they must eat the foods which are staple products of the zone in which they live. It is impossible to supply all the people with a nut-and-fruit or raw food diet; and the fact that it is impossible is proof positive that these are not the foods intended by nature, for nature, being formed for the advancement of life, has not made the obtaining of the means of life an impossibility. So, I say, the question, What shall I eat? has been answered for you. Eat wheat, corn, rye, oats, barley, buckwheat; eat vegetables; eat meats, eat fruits, eat the things that are eaten by the masses of the people around the world, for in this matter the voice of the people is the voice of God. They have been led, generally, to the selection of certain foods; and they have been led, generally, to prepare these foods in generally similar ways; and you may depend upon it that in general they have the right foods and are preparing them in the right way. In these matters the race has been under the guidance of God. The list of foods in common use is a long one, and you must select therefrom according to your individual taste; if you do, you will find that you have an infallible guide, as shown in the next two chapters.

If you do not eat until you have an EARNED hunger, you will not find your taste demanding unnatural or unhealthy foods. The woodchopper, who has swung his axe continuously from seven in the morning until noon does not come in clamoring for cream puffs and confectionery; he wants pork and beans, or beefsteak and potatoes, or corn bread and cabbage; he asks for the plain solids. Offer to crack him a few walnuts and give him a plate of lettuce, and you will be met with huge disdain; those things are not natural foods for a workingman. And if they are not natural foods for a workingman, they are not for any other man; for work hunger is the only real hunger, and requires the same materials to satisfy it, whether it be in woodchopper or banker, in man, woman or child.

It is a mistake to suppose that food must be selected with anxious care to fit the vocation of the person who eats. It is not true that the woodchopper requires "heavy" or "solid" foods and the bookkeeper "light" foods. If you are a bookkeeper, or other brain worker, and do not eat until you have an EARNED hunger, you will want exactly the same foods that the woodchopper wants. Your body is made of exactly the same elements as that of the woodchopper, and requires the same materials for cell-building; why, then, feed him on ham and eggs and corn bread and you on crackers and toast? True, most of his waste is of muscle, while most of yours is of brain and nerve tissue; but it is also true that the woodchopper's diet contains all the requisites for brain and nerve building in far better proportions than they are found in most "light" foods. The world's best brain work has been done on the fare of the working people. The world's greatest thinkers have invariably lived on the plain solid foods common among the masses.

Let the bookkeeper wait until he has an earned hunger before he eats; and then, if he wants ham, eggs, and corn bread, by all means let him eat them; but let him remember that he does not need one-twentieth of the amount necessary for the woodchopper. It is not eating "hearty" foods which gives the brain worker indigestion; it is eating as much as would be needed by a muscle worker. Indigestion is never caused by eating to satisfy hunger; it is always caused by eating to gratify appetite. If you eat in the manner prescribed in the next chapter, your taste will soon become so natural that you will never WANT anything that you cannot eat with impunity; and you can drop the whole anxious question of what to eat from your mind forever, and simply eat what you want. Indeed, that is the only way to do it if you are to think no thoughts but those of health; for you cannot think health so long as you are in continual doubt and uncertainty as to whether you are getting the right bills of fare.

"Take no thought what ye shall eat," said Jesus, and he spoke wisely. The foods found on the table of any ordinary middle-class or working class family will nourish your body perfectly if you eat at the right times and in the right way. If you want meat, eat it; and if you do not want it, do not eat it, and do not suppose that you must find some special substitute for it. You can live perfectly well on what is left on any table after the meat has been removed.

It is not necessary to worry about a "varied" diet, so as to get in all the necessary elements. The Chinese and Hindus build very good bodies and excellent brains on a diet of few variations, rice making almost the whole of it. The Scotch are physically and mentally strong on oatmeal cakes; and the Irishman is husky of body and brilliant of mind on potatoes and pork. The wheat berry contains practically all that is necessary for the building of brain and body; and a man can live very well on a monodiet of navy beans.

Form a conception of perfect health for yourself, and do not hold any thought which is not a thought of health.

NEVER eat until you have an EARNED HUNGER. Remember that it will not hurt you in the least to go hungry for a short time; but it will surely hurt you to eat when you are not hungry.

Do not give the least thought to what you should or should not eat; simply eat what is set before you, selecting that which pleases your taste most. In other words, eat what you want. This you can do with perfect results if you eat in the right way; and how to do this will be explained in the next chapter.

Chapter 11
How to Eat

It is a settled fact that man naturally chews his food. The few faddists who maintain that we should bolt our nourishment, after the manner of the dog and others of the lower animals, can no longer get a hearing; we know that we should chew our food. And if it is natural that we should chew our food, the more thoroughly we chew it the more completely natural the process must be. If you will chew every mouthful to a liquid, you need not be in the least concerned as to what you shall eat, for you can get sufficient nourishment out of any ordinary food.

Whether or not this chewing shall be an irksome and laborious task or a most enjoyable process, depends upon the mental attitude in which you come to the table.

If your mind and attitude are on other things, or if you are anxious or worried about business or domestic affairs, you will find it almost impossible to eat without bolting more or less of your food. You must learn to live so scientifically that you will have no business or domestic cares to worry about; this you can do, and you can also learn to give your undivided attention to the act of eating while at the table.

When you eat, do so with an eye single to the purpose of getting all the enjoyment you can from that meal; dismiss everything else from your mind, and do not let anything take your attention from the food and its taste until your meal is finished. Be cheerfully confident, for if you follow these instructions you may KNOW that the food you eat is exactly the right food, and that it will "agree" with you to perfection.

Sit down to the table with confident cheerfulness, and take a moderate portion of the food; take whatever thing looks most desirable to you. Do not select some food because you think it will be good for you; select that which will taste good to you. If you are to get well and stay well, you must drop the idea of doing things because they are good for your health, and do things because you want to do them. Select the food you want most; gratefully give thanks to God that you have learned how to eat it in such a way that digestion shall be perfect; and take a moderate mouthful of it.

Do not fix your attention on the act of chewing; fix it on the TASTE of the food; and taste and enjoy it until it is reduced to a liquid state and passes down your throat by involuntary swallowing. No matter how long it takes, do not think of the time. Think of the taste. Do not allow your eyes to wander over the table, speculating as to what you shall eat next; do not worry for fear there is not enough, and that you will not get your share of everything. Do not anticipate the taste of the next thing; keep your mind centered on the taste of what you have in your mouth. And that is all of it.

Scientific and healthful eating is a delightful process after you have learned how to do it, and after you have overcome the bad old habit of gobbling down your food unchewed. It is best not to have too much conversation going on while eating; be cheerful, but not talkative; do the talking afterward.

In most cases, some use of the will is required to form the habit of correct eating. The bolting habit is an unnatural one, and is without doubt mostly the result of fear. Fear that we will be robbed of our food; fear that we will not get our share of the good things; fear that we will lose precious time — these are the causes of haste. Then there is anticipation of the dainties that are to come for dessert, and the consequent desire to get at them as quickly as possible; and there is mental abstraction, or thinking of other matters while eating. All these must be overcome.

When you find that your mind is wandering, call a halt; think for a moment of the food, and of how good it tastes; of the perfect digestion and assimilation that are going to follow the meal, and begin again. Begin again and again, though you must do so twenty times in the course of a single meal; and again and again, though you must do so every meal for weeks and months. It is perfectly certain that you CAN form the "Fletcher habit" if you persevere; and when you have formed it, you will experience a healthful pleasure you have never known.

This is a vital point, and I must not leave it until I have thoroughly impressed it upon your mind. Given the right materials, perfectly prepared, the Principle of Health will positively build you a perfectly healthy body; and you cannot prepare the materials perfectly in any other way that the one I am describing. If you are to have perfect health, you MUST eat in just this way; you can, and the doing of it is only a matter of a little perseverance. What use for you to talk of mental control unless you will govern yourself in so simple a matter as ceasing to bolt your food? What use to talk of concentration unless you can keep your mind on the act of eating for so short a space as fifteen or twenty minutes, especially with all the pleasures of taste to help you? Go on, and conquer. In a few weeks, or months, as the case may be, you will find the habit of scientific eating becoming fixed; and soon you will be in so splendid a condition, mentally and physically, that nothing would induce you to return to the bad old way.

We have seen that if man will think only thoughts of perfect health, his internal functions will be performed in a healthy manner; and we have seen that in order to think thoughts of health, man must perform the voluntary functions in a healthy manner. The most important of the voluntary functions is that of eating; and we see, so far, no especial difficulty in eating in a perfectly healthy way. I will here summarize the instructions as to when to eat, what to eat, and how to eat, with the reasons therefor:

NEVER eat until you have an EARNED hunger, no matter how long you go without food. This is based on the fact that whenever food is needed in the system, if there is power to digest it, the sub-conscious mind announces the need by the sensation of hunger. Learn to distinguish between genuine hunger and the gnawing and craving sensations caused by unnatural appetite. Hunger is never a disagreeable feeling, accompanied by weakness, faintness, or gnawing feelings at the stomach; it is a pleasant, anticipatory desire for food, and is felt mostly in the mouth and throat. It does not come at certain hours or at stated intervals; it only comes when the sub-conscious mind is ready to receive, digest, and assimilate food.

Eat whatever foods you want, making your selection from the staples in general use in the zone in which you live. The Supreme Intelligence has guided man to the selection of these foods, and they are the right ones for all. I am referring, of course, to the foods which are taken to satisfy hunger, not to those which have been contrived merely to gratify appetite or perverted taste. The instinct which has guided the masses of men to make use of the great staples of food to satisfy their hunger is a divine one. God has made no mistake; if you eat these foods you will not go wrong.

Eat your food with cheerful confidence, and get all the pleasure that is to be had from the taste of every mouthful. Chew each morsel to a liquid, keeping your attention fixed on the enjoyment of the process. This is the only way to eat in a perfectly complete and successful manner; and when anything is done in a completely successful manner, the general result cannot be a failure. In the attainment of health, the law is the same as in the attainment of riches; if you make each act a success in itself, the sum of all your acts must be a success. When you eat in the mental attitude I have described, and in the manner I have described, nothing can be added to the process; it is done in a perfect manner, and it is successfully done. And if eating is successfully done, digestion, assimilation, and the building of a healthy body are successfully begun. We next take up the question of the quantity of food required.

Chapter 12
Hunger and Appetites

It is very easy to find the correct answer to the question, How much shall I eat? You are never to eat until you have an earned hunger, and you are to stop eating the instant you BEGIN to feel that your hunger is abating. Never gorge yourself; never eat to repletion. When you begin to feel that your hunger is satisfied, know that you have enough; for until you have enough, you will continue to feel the sensation of hunger. If you eat as directed in the last chapter, it is probable that you will begin to feel satisfied before you have taken half your usual amount; but stop there, all the same. No matter how delightfully attractive the dessert, or how tempting the pie or pudding, do not eat a mouthful of it if you find that your hunger has been in the least degree assuaged by the other foods you have taken.

Whatever you eat after your hunger begins to abate is taken to gratify taste and appetite, not hunger and is not called for by nature at all. It is therefore excess, mere debauchery, and it cannot fail to work mischief.

This is a point you will need to watch with nice discrimination, for the habit of eating purely for sensual gratification is very deeply rooted with most of us. The usual "dessert" of sweet and tempting foods is prepared solely with a view to inducing people to eat after hunger has been satisfied; and all the effects are evil. It is not that pie and cake are unwholesome foods; they are usually perfectly wholesome if eaten to satisfy hunger, and NOT to gratify appetite. If you want pie, cake, pastry, or puddings, it is better to begin your meal with them, finishing with the plainer and less tasty foods. You will find, however, that if you eat as directed in the preceding chapters, the plainest food will soon come to taste like kingly fare to you; for your sense of taste, like all your other senses, will become so acute with the general improvement in your condition that you will find new delights in common things. No glutton ever enjoyed a meal like the man who eats for hunger only, who gets the most out of every mouthful, and who stops on the instant that he feels the edge taken from his hunger. The first intimation that hunger is abating is the signal from the sub-conscious mind that it is time to quit.

The average person who takes up this plan of living will be greatly surprised to learn how little food is really required to keep the body in perfect condition. The amount depends upon the work; upon how much muscular exercise is taken, and upon the extent to which the person is exposed to cold. The woodchopper who goes into the forest in the winter time and swings his axe all day can eat two full meals; but the brain worker who sits all day on a chair, in a warm room, does not need one third and often not one tenth as much. Most woodchoppers eat two or three times as much, and most brain workers from three to ten times as much as nature calls for; and the elimination of this vast amount of surplus rubbish from their systems is a tax on vital power which in time depletes their energy and leaves them an easy prey to so-called disease. Get all possible enjoyment out of the taste of your food, but never eat anything merely because it tastes good; and on the instant that you feel that your hunger is less keen, stop eating.

If you will consider for a moment, you will see that there is positively no other way for you to settle these various food questions than by adopting the plan here laid down for you. As to the proper time to eat, there is no other way to decide than to say that you should eat whenever you have an EARNED HUNGER. It is a self-evident proposition that that is the right time to eat, and that any other is a wrong time to eat. As to what to eat, the Eternal Wisdom has decided that the masses of men shall eat the staple products of the zones in which they live. The staple foods of your particular zone are the right foods for you; and the Eternal Wisdom, working in and through the minds of the masses of men, has taught them how best to prepare these foods by cooking and otherwise. And as to how to eat, you know that you must chew your food; and if it must be chewed, then reason tells us that the more thorough and perfect the operation the better.

I repeat that success in anything is attained by making each separate act a success in itself. If you make each action, however small and unimportant, a thoroughly successful action, your day's work as a whole cannot result in failure. If you make the actions of each day successful, the sum total of your life cannot be failure. A great success is the result of doing a large number of little things, and doing each one in a perfectly successful way. If every thought is a healthy thought, and if every action of your life is performed in a healthy way, you must soon attain to perfect health. It is impossible to devise a way in which you can perform the act of eating more successfully, and in a manner more in accord with the laws of life, than by chewing every mouthful to a liquid, enjoying the taste fully, and keeping a cheerful confidence all the while. Nothing can be added to make the process more successful; while if anything be subtracted, the process will not be a completely healthy one.

In the matter of how much to eat, you will also see that there could be no other guide so natural, so safe, and so reliable as the one I have prescribed — to stop eating on the instant you feel that your hunger begins to abate. The sub-conscious mind may be trusted with implicit reliance to inform us when food is needed; and it may be trusted as implicitly to inform us when the need has been supplied. If ALL food is eaten for hunger, and NO food is taken merely to gratify taste, you will never eat too much; and if you eat whenever you have an EARNED hunger, you will always eat enough. By reading carefully the summing up in the following chapter, you will see that the requirements for eating in a perfectly healthy way are really very few and simple.

The matter of drinking in a natural way may be dismissed here with a very few words. If you wish to be exactly and rigidly scientific, drink nothing but water; drink only when you are thirsty; drink whenever you are thirsty, and stop as soon as you feel that your thirst begins to abate. But if you are living rightly in regard to eating, it will not be necessary to practice asceticism or great self-denial in the matter of drinking. You can take an occasional cup of weak coffee without harm; you can, to a reasonable extent, follow the customs of those around you. Do not get the soda fountain habit; do not drink merely to tickle your palate with sweet liquids; be sure that you take a drink of water whenever you feel thirst. Never be too lazy, too indifferent, or too busy to get a drink of water when you feel the least thirst; if you obey this rule, you will have little inclination to take strange and unnatural drinks. Drink only to satisfy thirst; drink whenever you feel thirst; and stop drinking as soon as you feel thirst abating. That is the perfectly healthy way to supply the body with the necessary fluid material for its internal processes.

Chapter 13
In a Nutshell

There is a Cosmic Life which permeates, penetrates, and fills the interspaces of the universe, being in and through all things. This Life is not merely a vibration, or form of energy; it is a Living Substance. All things are made from it; it is All, and in all.

This Substance thinks, and it assumes the form of that which it thinks about. The thought of a form, in this substance, creates the form; the thought of a motion institutes the motion. The visible universe, with all its forms and motions, exists because it is in the thought of Original Substance.

Man is a form of Original Substance, and can think original thoughts; and within himself, man's thoughts have controlling or formative power. The thought of a condition produces that condition; the thought of a motion institutes that motion. So long as man thinks of the conditions and motions of disease, so long will the conditions and motions of disease exist within him. If man will think only of perfect health, the Principle of Health within him will maintain normal conditions.

To be well, man must form a conception of perfect health, and hold thoughts harmonious with that conception as regards himself and all things. He must think only of healthy conditions and functioning; he must not permit a thought of unhealthy or abnormal conditions or functioning to find lodgment in his mind at any time.

In order to think only of healthy conditions and functioning, man must perform the voluntary acts of life in a perfectly healthy way. He cannot think perfect health so long as he knows that he is living in a wrong or unhealthy way; or even so long as he has doubts as to whether or not he is living in a healthy way. Man cannot think thoughts of perfect health while his voluntary functions are performed in the manner of one who is sick. The voluntary functions of life are eating, drinking, breathing, and sleeping. When man thinks only of healthy conditions and functioning, and performs these externals in a perfectly healthy manner, he must have perfect health.

In eating, man must learn to be guided by his hunger. He must distinguish between hunger and appetite, and between hunger and the cravings of habit; he must NEVER eat unless he feels an EARNED HUNGER. He must learn that genuine hunger is never present after natural sleep, and that the demand for an early morning meal is purely a matter of habit and appetite; and he must not begin his day by eating in violation of natural law. He must wait until he has an Earned Hunger, which, in most cases, will make his first meal come at about the noon hour. No matter what his condition, vocation, or circumstances, he must make it his rule not to eat until he has an EARNED HUNGER; and he may remember that it is far better to fast for several hours after he has become hungry than to eat before he begins to feel hunger. It will not hurt you to go hungry for a few hours, even though you are working hard; but it will hurt you to fill your stomach when you are not hungry, whether you are working or not. If you never eat until you have an Earned Hunger, you may be certain that in so far as the time of eating is concerned, you are proceeding in a perfectly healthy way. This is a self-evident proposition.

As to what he shall eat, man must be guided by that Intelligence which has arranged that the people of any given portion of the earth's surface must live on the staple products of the zone which they inhabit. Have faith in God, and ignore "food science" of every kind. Do not pay the slightest attention to the controversies as to the relative merits of cooked and raw foods; of vegetables and meats; or as to your need for carbohydrates and proteins. Eat only when you have an earned hunger, and then take the common foods of the masses of the people in the zone in which you live, and have perfect confidence that the results will be good. They will be. Do not seek for luxuries, or for things imported or fixed up to tempt the taste; stick to the plain solids; and when these do not "taste good," fast until they do. Do not seek for "light" foods; for easily digestible, or "healthy" foods; eat what the farmers and workingmen eat. Then you will be functioning in a perfectly healthy manner, so far as what to eat is concerned. I repeat, if you have no hunger or taste for the plain foods, do not eat at all; wait until hunger comes. Go without eating until the plainest food tastes good to you; and then begin your meal with what you like best.

In deciding how to eat, man must be guided by reason. We can see that the abnormal states of hurry and worry produced by wrong thinking about business and similar things have led us to form the habit of eating too fast, and chewing too little. Reason tells us that food should be chewed, and that the more thoroughly it is chewed the better it is prepared for the chemistry of digestion. Furthermore, we can see that the man who eats slowly and chews his food to a liquid, keeping his mind on the process and giving it his undivided attention, will enjoy more of the pleasure of taste than he who bolts his food with his mind on something else. To eat in a perfectly healthy manner, man must concentrate his attention on the act, with cheerful enjoyment and confidence; he must taste his food, and he must reduce each mouthful to a liquid before swallowing it. The foregoing instructions, if followed, make the function of eating completely perfect; nothing can be added as to what, when, and how.

In the matter of how much to eat, man must be guided by the same inward intelligence, or Principle of Health, which tells him when food is wanted. He must stop eating in the moment that he feels hunger abating; he must not eat beyond this point to gratify taste. If he ceases to eat in the instant that the inward demand for food ceases, he will never overeat; and the function of supplying the body with food will be performed in a perfectly healthy manner.

The matter of eating naturally is a very simple one; there is nothing in all the foregoing that cannot be easily practiced by any one. This method, put in practice, will infallibly result in perfect digestion and assimilation; and all anxiety and careful thought concerning the matter can at once be dropped from the mind. Whenever you have an earned hunger, eat with thankfulness what is set before you, chewing each mouthful to a liquid, and stopping when you feel the edge taken from your hunger.

The importance of the mental attitude is sufficient to justify an additional word. While you are eating, as at all other times, think only of healthy conditions and normal functioning. Enjoy what you eat; if you carry on a conversation at the table, talk of the goodness of the food, and of the pleasure it is giving you. Never mention that you dislike this or that; speak only of those things which you like. Never discuss the wholesomeness or unwholesomeness of foods; never mention or think of unwholesomeness at all. If there is anything on the table for which you do not care, pass it by in silence, or with a word of commendation; never criticize or object to anything. Eat your food with gladness and with singleness of heart, praising God and giving thanks. Let your watchword be perseverance; whenever you fall into the old way of hasty eating, or of wrong thought and speech, bring yourself up short and begin again.

It is of the most vital importance to you that you should be a self-controlling and self-directing person; and you can never hope to become so unless you can master yourself in so simple and fundamental a matter as the manner and method of your eating. If you cannot control yourself in this, you cannot control yourself in anything that will be worthwhile. On the other hand, if you carry out the foregoing instructions, you may rest in the assurance that in so far as right thinking and right eating are concerned you are living in a perfectly scientific way; and you may also be assured that if you practice what is prescribed in the following chapters you will quickly build your body into a condition of perfect health.

Chapter 14
Breathing

The function of breathing is a vital one, and it immediately concerns the continuance of life. We can live many hours without sleeping, and many days without eating or drinking, but only a few minutes without breathing. The act of breathing is involuntary, but the manner of it, and the provision of the proper conditions for its healthy performance, falls within the scope of volition. Man will continue to breathe involuntarily, but he can voluntarily determine what he shall breathe, and how deeply and thoroughly he shall breathe; and he can, of his own volition, keep the physical mechanism in condition for the perfect performance of the function.

It is essential, if you wish to breathe in a perfectly healthy way, that the physical machinery used in the act should be kept in good condition. You must keep your spine moderately straight, and the muscles of your chest must be flexible and free in action. You cannot breathe in the right way if your shoulders are greatly stooped forward and your chest hollow and rigid. Sitting or standing at work in a slightly stooping position tends to produce hollow chest; so does lifting heavy weights or light weights.

The tendency of work, of almost all kinds, is to pull the shoulders forward, curve the spine, and flatten the chest; and if the chest is greatly flattened, full and deep breathing becomes impossible, and perfect health is out of the question.

Various gymnastic exercises have been devised to counteract the effect of stooping while at work; such as hanging by the hands from a swing or trapeze bar, or sitting on a chair with the feet under some heavy article of furniture and bending backward until the head touches the floor, and so on. All these are good enough in their way, but very few people will follow them long enough and regularly enough to accomplish any real gain in physique. The taking of "health exercises" of any kind is burdensome and unnecessary; there is a more natural, simpler, and much better way.

This better way is to keep yourself straight, and to breathe deeply. Let your mental conception of yourself be that you are a perfectly straight person, and whenever the matter comes to your mind, be sure that you instantly expand your chest, throw back your shoulders, and "straighten up." Whenever you do this, slowly draw in your breath until you fill your lungs to their utmost capacity; "crowd in" all the air you possibly can; and while holding it for an instant in the lungs, throw your shoulders still further back, and stretch your chest; at the same time try to pull your spine forward between the shoulders. Then let the air go easily.

This is the one great exercise for keeping the chest full, flexible, and in good condition. Straighten up; fill your lungs FULL; stretch your chest and straighten your spine, and exhale easily. And this exercise you must repeat, in season and out of season, at all times and in all places, until you form a habit of doing it; you can easily do so. Whenever you step out of doors into the fresh, pure air, BREATHE. When you are at work, and think of yourself and your position, BREATHE. When you are in company, and are reminded of the matter, BREATHE. When you are awake in the night, BREATHE. No matter where you are or what you are doing, whenever the idea comes to your mind, straighten up and BREATHE. If you walk to and from your work, take the exercise all the way; it will soon become a delight to you; you will keep it up, not for the sake of health, but as a matter of pleasure.

Do not consider this a "health exercise"; never take health exercises, or do gymnastics to make you well. To do so is to recognize sickness as a present fact or as a possibility, which is precisely what you must not do. The people who are always taking exercises for their health are always thinking about being sick. It ought to be a matter of pride with you to keep your spine straight and strong; as much so as it is to keep your face clean. Keep your spine straight, and your chest full and flexible for the same reason that you keep your hands clean and your nails manicured; because it is slovenly to do otherwise. Do it without a thought of sickness, present or possible. You must either be crooked and unsightly, or you must be straight; and if you are straight your breathing will take care of itself. You will find the matter of health exercises referred to again in a future chapter.

It is essential, however, that you should breathe AIR. It appears to be the intention of nature that the lungs should receive air containing its regular percentage of oxygen, and not greatly contaminated by other gases, or by filth of any kind. Do not allow yourself to think that you are compelled to live or work where the air is not fit to breathe. If your house cannot be properly ventilated, move; and if you are employed where the air is bad, get another job; you can, by practicing the methods given in the preceding volume of this series, "THE SCIENCE OF GETTING RICH." If no one would consent to work in bad air, employers would speedily see to it that all work rooms were properly ventilated. The worst air is that from which the oxygen has been exhausted by breathing; as that of churches and theaters where crowds of people congregate, and the outlet and supply of air are poor. Next to this is air containing other gases than oxygen and hydrogen — sewer gas, and the effluvium from decaying things. Air that is heavily charged with dust or particles of organic matter may be endured better than any of these. Small particles of organic matter other than food are generally thrown off from the lungs; but gases go into the blood.

I speak advisedly when I say "other than food." Air is largely a food. It is the most thoroughly alive thing we take into the body. Every breath carries in millions of microbes, many of which are assimilated. The odors from earth, grass, tree, flower, plant, and from cooking foods are foods in themselves; they are minute particles of the substances from which they come, and are often so attenuated that they pass directly from the lungs into the blood, and are assimilated without digestion. And the atmosphere is permeated with the One Original Substance, which is life itself. Consciously recognize this whenever you think of your breathing, and think that you are breathing in life; you really are, and conscious recognition helps the process. See to it that you do not breathe air containing poisonous gases, and that you do not rebreathe the air which has been used by yourself or others.

That is all there is to the matter of breathing correctly. Keep your spine straight and your chest flexible, and breathe pure air, recognizing with thankfulness the fact that you breathe in the Eternal Life. That is not difficult; and beyond these things give little thought to your breathing except to thank God that you have learned how to do it perfectly.

Chapter 15
Sleep

Vital power is renewed in sleep. Every living thing sleeps; men, animals, reptiles, fish, and insects sleep, and even plants have regular periods of slumber. And this is because it is in sleep that we come into such contact with the Principle of Life in nature that our own lives may be renewed. It is in sleep that the brain of man is recharged with vital energy, and the Principle of Health within him is given new strength. It is of the first importance, then, that we should sleep in a natural, normal, and perfectly healthy manner.

Studying sleep, we note that the breathing is much deeper, and more forcible and rhythmic than in the waking state. Much more air is inspired when asleep than when awake, and this tells us that the Principle of Health requires large quantities of some element in the atmosphere for the process of renewal. If you would surround sleep with natural conditions, then, the first step is to see that you have an unlimited supply of fresh and pure air to breathe. Physicians have found that sleeping in the pure air of out-of-doors is very efficacious in the treatment of pulmonary troubles; and, taken in connection with the Way of Living and Thinking prescribed in this book, you will find that it is just as efficacious in curing every other sort of trouble. Do not take any half-way measures in this matter of securing pure air while you sleep. Ventilate your bedroom thoroughly; so thoroughly that it will be practically the same as sleeping out of doors. Have a door or window open wide; have one open on each side of the room, if possible. If you cannot have a good draft of air across the room, pull the head of your bed close to the open window, so that the air from without may come fully into your face. No matter how cold or unpleasant the weather, have a window open, and open wide; and try to get a circulation of pure air through the room. Pile on the bedclothes, if necessary, to keep you warm; but have an unlimited supply of fresh air from out of doors. This is the first great requisite for healthy sleep.

The brain and nerve centers cannot be thoroughly vitalized if you sleep in "dead" or stagnant air; you must have the living atmosphere, vital with nature's Principle of Life. I repeat, do not make any compromise in this matter; ventilate your sleeping room completely, and see that there is a circulation of outdoor air through it while you sleep. You are not sleeping in a perfectly healthy way if you shut the doors and windows of your sleeping room, whether in winter or summer. Have fresh air. If you are where there is no fresh air, move. If your bedroom cannot be ventilated, get into another house.

Next in importance is the mental attitude in which you go to sleep. It is well to sleep intelligently, purposefully, knowing what you do it for. Lie down thinking that sleep is an infallible vitalizer, and go to sleep with a confident faith that your strength is to be renewed; that you will awake full of vitality and health. Put purpose into your sleep as you do into your eating; give the matter your attention for a few minutes, as you go to rest. Do not seek your couch with a discouraged or depressed feeling; go there joyously, to be made whole. Do not forget the exercise of gratitude in going to sleep; before you close your eyes, give thanks to God for having shown you the way to perfect health, and go to sleep with this grateful thought uppermost in your mind. A bedtime prayer of thanksgiving is a mighty good thing; it puts the Principle of Health within you into communication with its source, from which it is to receive new power while you are in the silence of unconsciousness.

You may see that the requirements for perfectly healthy sleep are not difficult. First, to see that you breathe pure air from out-of-doors while you sleep; and, second, to put the Within into touch with the Living Substance by a few minutes of grateful meditation as you go to bed. Observe these requirements, go to sleep in a thankful and confident frame of mind, and all will be well. If you have insomnia, do not let it worry you. While you lie awake, form your conception of health; meditate with thankfulness on the abundant life which is yours, breathe, and feel perfectly confident that you will sleep in due time; and you will. Insomnia, like every other ailment, must give way before the Principle of Health aroused to full constructive activity by the course of thought and action herein described.

The reader will now comprehend that it is not at all burdensome or disagreeable to perform the voluntary functions of life in a perfectly healthy way. The perfectly healthy way is the easiest, simplest, most natural, and most pleasant way. The cultivation of health is not a work of art, difficulty, or strenuous labor. You have only to lay aside artificial observances of every kind, and eat, drink, breathe, and sleep in the most natural and delightful way; and if you do this, thinking health and only health, you will certainly be well.

Chapter 16
Supplementary Instructions

In forming a conception of health, it is necessary to think of the manner in which you would live and work if you were perfectly well and very strong; to imagine yourself doing things in the way of a perfectly well and very strong person, until you have a fairly good conception of what you would be if you were well. Then take a mental and physical attitude in harmony with this conception; and do not depart from this attitude. You must unify yourself in thought with the thing you desire; and whatever state or condition you unify with yourself in thought will soon become unified with you in body. The scientific way is to sever relations with everything you do not want, and to enter into relations with everything you do want. Form a conception of perfect health, and relate yourself to this conception in word, act, and attitude.

Guard your speech; make every word harmonize with the conception of perfect health. Never complain; never say things like these: "I did not sleep well last night;" "I have a pain in my side;" "I do not feel at all well today," and so on. Say "I am looking forward to a good night's sleep to-night;" "I can see that I progress rapidly," and things of similar meaning. In so far as everything which is connected with disease is concerned, your way is to forget it; and in so far as everything which is connected with health is concerned, your way is to unify yourself with it in thought and speech.

This is the whole thing in a nutshell: Make yourself one with Health in thought, word, and action; and do not connect yourself with sickness either by thought, word, or action.

Do not read "Doctor Books" or medical literature, or the literature of those whose theories conflict with those herein set forth; to do so will certainly undermine your faith in the Way of Living upon which you have entered, and cause you to again come into mental relations with disease. This book really gives you all that is required; nothing essential has been omitted, and practically all the superfluous has been eliminated. The Science of Being Well is an exact science, like arithmetic; nothing can be added to the fundamental principles, and if anything be taken from them, a failure will result. If you follow strictly the way of living prescribed in this book, you will be well; and you certainly CAN follow this way, both in thought and action.

Relate not only yourself, but so far as possible all others, in your thoughts, to perfect health. Do not sympathize with people when they complain, or even when they are sick and suffering. Turn their thoughts into a constructive channel if you can; do all you can for their relief, but do it with the health thought in your mind. Do not let people tell their woes and catalogue their symptoms to you; turn the conversation to some other subject, or excuse yourself and go. Better be considered an unfeeling person than to have the disease thought forced upon you. When you are in company of people whose conversational stock-in-trade is sickness and kindred matters, ignore what they say and fall to offering a mental prayer of gratitude for your perfect health; and if that does not enable you to shut out their thoughts, say goodbye and leave them. No matter what they think or say; politeness does not require you to permit yourself to be poisoned by diseased or perverted thought. When we have a few more hundreds of thousands of enlightened thinkers who will not stay where people complain and talk sickness, the world will advance rapidly toward health. When you let people talk to you of sickness, you assist them to increase and multiply sickness.

What shall I do when I am in pain? Can one be in actual physical suffering and still think only thoughts of health?

Yes. Do not resist pain; recognize that it is a good thing. Pain is caused by an effort of the Principle of Health to overcome some unnatural condition; this you must know and feel. When you have a pain, think that a process of healing is going on in the affected part, and mentally assist and co-operate with it. Put yourself in full mental harmony with the power which is causing the pain; assist it; help it along. Do not hesitate, when necessary, to use hot fomentations and similar means to further the good work which is going on. If the pain is severe, lie down and give your mind to the work of quietly and easily co-operating with the force which is at work for your good. This is the time to exercise gratitude and faith; be thankful for the power of health which is causing the pain, and be certain that the pain will cease as soon as the good work is done. Fix your thoughts, with confidence, on the Principle of Health which is making such conditions within you that pain will soon be unnecessary. You will be surprised to find how easily you can conquer pain; and after you have lived for a time in this Scientific Way, pains and aches will be things unknown to you.

What shall I do when I am too weak for my work? Shall I drive myself beyond my strength, trusting in God to support me? Shall I go on, like the runner, expecting a "second wind"?

No; better not. When you begin to live in this Way, you will probably not be of normal strength; and you will gradually pass from a low physical condition to a higher one. If you relate yourself mentally with health and strength, and perform the voluntary functions of life in a perfectly healthy manner, your strength will increase from day to day; but for a time you may have days when your strength is insufficient for the work you would like to do. At such times rest, and exercise gratitude. Recognize the fact that your strength is growing rapidly, and feel a deep thankfulness to the Living One from whom it comes.

Spend an hour of weakness in thanksgiving and rest, with full faith that great strength is at hand; and then get up and go on again. While you rest do not think of your present weakness; think of the strength that is coming.

Never, at any time, allow yourself to think that you are giving way to weakness; when you rest, as when you go to sleep, fix your mind on the Principle of Health which is building you into complete strength.

What shall I do about that great bugaboo which scares millions of people to death every year — Constipation?

Do nothing. Read Horace Fletcher on "The A B Z or Our Own Nutrition," and get the full force of his explanation of the fact that when you live on this scientific plan you need not, and indeed cannot, have an evacuation of the bowels every day; and that an operation in from once in three days to once in two weeks is quite sufficient for perfect health. The gross feeders who eat from three to ten times as much as can be utilized in their systems have a great amount of waste to eliminate; but if you live in the manner we have described it will be otherwise with you.

If you eat only when you have an EARNED HUNGER, and chew every mouthful to a liquid, and if you stop eating the instant you BEGIN to be conscious of an abatement of your hunger, you will so perfectly prepare your food for digestion and assimilation that practically all of it will be taken up by the absorbents; and there will be little — almost nothing — remaining in the bowels to be excreted. If you are able to entirely banish from your memory all that you have read in "doctor books" and patent medicine advertisements concerning constipation, you need give the matter no further thought at all. The Principle of Health will take care of it.

But if your mind has been filled with fear-thought in regard to constipation, it may be well in the beginning for you to occasionally flush the colon with warm water. There is not the least need of doing it, except to make the process of your mental emancipation from fear a little easier; it may be worthwhile for that. And as soon as you see that you are making good progress, and that you have cut down your quantity of food, and are really eating in the Scientific Way, dismiss constipation from your mind forever; you have nothing more to do with it. Put your trust in that Principle within you which has the power to give you perfect health; relate It by your reverent gratitude to the Principle of Life which is All Power, and go on your way rejoicing.

What about exercise?

Every one is the better for a little all-round use of the muscles every day; and the best way to get this is to do it by engaging in some form of play or amusement. Get your exercise in the natural way; as recreation, not as a forced stunt for health's sake alone. Ride a horse or a bicycle; play tennis or tenpins, or toss a ball. Have some avocation like gardening in which you can spend an hour every day with pleasure and profit; there are a thousand ways in which you can get exercise enough to keep your body supple and your circulation good, and yet not fall into the rut of "exercising for your health." Exercise for fun or profit; exercise because you are too healthy to sit still, and not because you wish to become healthy, or to remain so.

Are long continued fasts necessary?

Seldom, if ever. The Principle of Health does not often require twenty, thirty, or forty days to get ready for action; under normal conditions, hunger will come in much less time. In most long fasts, the reason hunger does not come sooner is because it has been inhibited by the patient himself. He begins the fast with the FEAR if not actually with the hope that it will be many days before hunger comes; the literature he has read on the subject has prepared him to expect a long fast, and he is grimly determined to go to a finish, let the time be as long as it will. And the sub-conscious mind, under the influence of powerful and positive suggestion, suspends hunger.

When, for any reason, nature takes away your hunger, go cheerfully on with your usual work, and do not eat until she gives it back. No matter if it is two, three, ten days, or longer; you may be perfectly sure that when it is time for you to eat you will be hungry; and if you are cheerfully confident and keep your faith in health, you will suffer from no weakness or discomfort caused by abstinence. When you are not hungry, you will feel stronger, happier, and more comfortable if you do not eat than you will if you do eat; no matter how long the fast. And if you live in the scientific way described in this book, you will never have to take long fasts; you will seldom miss a meal, and you will enjoy your meals more than ever before in your life. Get an earned hunger before you eat; and whenever you get an earned hunger, eat.

Chapter 17
A Summary of The Science of Being Well

Health is perfectly natural functioning, normal living. There is a Principle of Life in the universe; it is the Living Substance, from which all things are made. This Living Substance permeates, penetrates, and fills the interspaces of the universe. In its invisible state it is in and through all forms; and yet all forms are made of it. To illustrate: Suppose that a very fine and highly diffusible aqueous vapor should permeate and penetrate a block of ice. The ice is formed from living water, and is living water in form; while the vapor is also living water, unformed, permeating a form made from itself. This illustration will explain how Living Substance permeates all forms made from It; all life comes from It; it is all the life there is.

This Universal Substance is a thinking substance, and takes the form of its thought. The thought of a form, held by it, creates the form; and the thought of a motion causes the motion. It cannot help thinking, and so is forever creating; and it must move on toward fuller and more complete expression of itself. This means toward more complete life and more perfect functioning; and that means toward perfect health.

The power of the living substance must always be exerted toward perfect health; it is a force in all things making for perfect functioning.

All things are permeated by a power which makes for health.

Man can relate himself to this power, and ally himself with it; he can also separate himself from it in his thoughts.

Man is a form of this Living Substance, and has within him a Principle of Health. This Principle of Health, when in full constructive activity, causes all the involuntary functions of man's body to be perfectly performed.

Man is a thinking substance, permeating a visible body, and the processes of his body are controlled by his thought.

When man thinks only thoughts of perfect health, the internal processes of his body will be those of perfect health. Man's first step toward perfect health must be to form a conception of himself as perfectly healthy, and as doing all things in the way and manner of a perfectly healthy person. Having formed this conception, he must relate himself to it in all his thoughts, and sever all thought relations with disease and weakness.

If he does this, and thinks his thoughts of health with positive FAITH, man will cause the Principle of Health within him to become constructively active, and to heal all his diseases. He can receive additional power from the universal Principle of Life by faith, and he can acquire faith by looking to this Principle of Life with reverent gratitude for the health it gives him. If man will consciously accept the health which is being continually given to him by the Living Substance, and if he will be duly grateful therefor, he will develop faith.

Man cannot think only thoughts of perfect health unless he performs the voluntary functions of life in a perfectly healthy manner. These voluntary functions are eating, drinking, breathing, and sleeping. If man thinks only thoughts of health, has faith in health, and eats, drinks, breathes, and sleeps in a perfectly healthy way, he must have perfect health.

Health is the result of thinking and acting in a Certain Way; and if a sick man begins to think and act in this Way, the Principle of Health within him will come into constructive activity and heal all his diseases. This Principle of Health is the same in all, and is related to the Life Principle of the universe; it is able to heal every disease, and will come into activity whenever man thinks and acts in accordance with the Science of Being Well. Therefore, every man can attain to perfect health.

How to Get What You Want: The Science of Being Successful

by Wallace D. Wattles

edited by Jeffrey L. King

Contents

1: Success is Within You 119
2: Using Your Higher Faculties to Overcome Self-Doubt 121
3: Making Use of Your Full Potential 123
4: Getting the Most Out of Life 126
5: The Science of Being Successful 129

Chapter 1
Success is Within You

Getting what you want is success; and success is an effect, coming from the application of a cause. Success is essentially the same in all cases; the difference is in the things the successful people want, but not in the success. Success is essentially the same, whether it results in the attainment of health, wealth, development or position; success is attainment, without regard to the things attained. And it is a law in nature that like causes always produce like effects; therefore, since success is the same in all cases, the cause of success must be the same in all cases.

The cause of success is always in the person who succeeds; you will see that this must be true, because if the cause of success were in nature, outside the person, then all persons similarly situated would succeed.

The cause of success is not in the environment of the individual, because if it were, all persons within a given radius would be successful, and success would be wholly a matter of neighborhood; and we see that people whose environments are practically the same, and who live in the same neighborhood show us all degrees of success and failure; therefore, we know that the cause of success must be in the individual, and nowhere else.

It is, therefore, mathematically certain that you can succeed if you will find out the cause of success, and develop it to sufficient strength, and apply it properly to your work; for the application of a sufficient cause cannot fail to produce a given effect. If there is a failure anywhere, of any kind, it is because the cause was either not sufficient or was not properly applied. The cause of success is some power within you; you have the power to develop any power to a limitless extent; for there is no end to mental growth; you can increase the strength of this power indefinitely, and so you can make it strong enough to do what you want to do, and to get what you want to get; when it is strong enough you can learn how to apply it to the work, and therefore, you can certainly succeed.

All you have to learn is what is the cause of success, and how it must be applied. The development of the special faculties to be used in your work is essential. We do not expect anyone to succeed as a musician without developing the musical faculty; and it would be absurd to expect a machinist to succeed without developing the mechanical faculty, a clergyman to succeed without developing spiritual understanding and the use of words, or a banker to succeed without developing the faculty of finance. And in choosing a business, you should choose the one which will call for the use of your strongest faculties. If you have good mechanical ability, and are not spiritually minded and have no command of language, do not try to preach; and if you have the taste and talent to combine colors and fabrics into beautiful creation in millinery and dress, do not learn typewriting or stenography; get into a business which will use your strongest faculties, and develop these faculties all you can; and even this is not enough to insure success.

There are people with fine musical talent who fail as musicians; with good mechanical ability who fail as carpenters, blacksmiths and machinists; with deep spirituality and fluent use of language who fail as clergymen; with keen and logical minds who fail as lawyers, and so on; the special faculties used in your work are the tools you use, but success does not depend alone on having good tools; it depends more on the power which uses and applies the tools. Be sure that your tools are the best and kept in the best condition; you can cultivate any faculty to any desired extent.

The application of the musical faculty causes success in music; that of the mechanical faculty causes success in mechanical pursuits; that of the financial faculty causes success in banking, and so on; and the something which applies these faculties, or causes them to be applied is the cause of success. The faculties are tools; the user of the tools is you, yourself; that in you which can cause you to use the tools in the right way, at the right time and in the right place is the cause of success.

What is this something in the person which causes him to use his faculties successfully? What it is and how to develop it will be fully explained in the next section; but before taking that up you should read this section over several times, so as to fix upon your mind the impregnable logic of the statement that you can succeed. You can; and if you study the foregoing argument well, you will be convinced that you can; and to become convinced that you can succeed is the first requisite to success.

Chapter 2
Using Your Higher Faculties to Overcome Self-Doubt

The faculties of the human mind are the tools with which success is attained, and the right application of these tools to your work or business will do it successfully and get what you want. A few people succeed because they use their faculties successfully, and the majority, who have equally good faculties, fail because they use them unsuccessfully.

There is something in the man who succeeds which enables him to use his faculties successfully, and this something must be cultivated by all who succeed; the question is, What is it? It is hard to find a word which shall express it, and not be misleading. This something is Poise; and poise is peace and power combined; but it is more than poise, for poise is a condition, and this something is an action as well as a condition. This Something is Faith; but it is more than faith, as faith is commonly understood: As commonly understood, faith consists in the action of believing things which cannot be proved; and the Something which causes success is more than that. It is Conscious Power in Action.

It is ACTIVE POWER-CONSCIOUSNESS.

Power-Consciousness is what you feel when you know that you can do a thing; and you know HOW to do the thing. If I can cause you to KNOW that you can succeed, and to know that you know HOW to succeed, I have placed success within your grasp; for if you know that you can do a thing and know that you know how to do it, it is impossible that you should fail to do it, if you really try. When you are in full Power-Consciousness, you will approach the task in an absolutely successful frame of mind. Every thought will be a successful thought, every action a successful action; and if every thought and action is successful, the sum-total of all your actions cannot be failure. What I have to do in these lessons, then, is to teach you how to create Power-Consciousness in yourself, so that you will know that you can do what you want to do and then to teach you how to do what you want to do.

Read again the preceding section; it proves by unanswerable logic that you CAN succeed. It shows that all that is in any mind is in your mind; the difference, if any, being in development. It is a fact in nature that the undeveloped is always capable of development; we see then that the cause of success is in you, and is capable of full development.

Having read this you must believe that it is possible for you to succeed; but it is not enough for you to believe that you can; you must know that you can; and the subconscious mind must know it as well as the objective mind. People have a way of saying, "he can who thinks he can"; but this is not true. It is not even true that he can who knows he can, if only the objective mind is spoken of; for the subconscious mind will often completely set aside and overcome what is positively known by the objective mind. It is a true statement, however, that he can whose subconscious mind knows that he can; and it is especially true if his objective mind has been trained to do the work.

People fail because they think, objectively, that they can do things, but do not know, subconsciously, that they can do them. It is more than likely that your subconscious mind is even now impressed with doubts of your ability to succeed; and these must be removed, or it will withhold its power when you need it most.

The subconscious mind is the source from which power comes in the action of any faculty; and a doubt will cause this power to be withheld, and the action will be weak; therefore, your first step must be to impress your subconscious mind with that fact that you CAN. This must be done by repeated suggestions. Practice the following mental exercise several times a day, and especially just before going to sleep; think quietly about the subconscious mentality, which permeates your whole body as water permeates a sponge; as you think of this mind, try to feel it; you will soon be able to become conscious of it. Hold this consciousness, and say with deep, earnest feeling: "I CAN succeed! All that is possible to anyone is possible to me. I AM successful. I do succeed, for I am full of the Power of Success." This is the simple truth. Realize that it is true, and repeat it over and over until your mentality is saturated through and through with the knowledge that YOU CAN DO WHAT YOU WANT TO DO. You can; other people have, and you can do more than anyone has ever done, for no one has ever yet used all the power that is capable of being used. It is within your power to make a greater success in your business than anyone has ever made before you. Practice the above autosuggestion for a month with persistence, and you will begin to KNOW that you have within you that which CAN do what you want to do; and then you will be ready for the next section which will tell you how to proceed in doing what you want to do. But remember that it is absolutely essential that you should first impress upon the subconscious mind the knowledge that you CAN.

Chapter 3
Making Use of Your Full Potential

Having filled your mentality, conscious and subconscious, with the faith that you CAN get what you want, the next question is one of the methods. You know that you can do it if you proceed in the right way; but which is the right way? This much is certain; to get more, you must make constructive use of what you have. You cannot use what you have not; therefore, your problem is how to make the most constructive use of what you already have. Do not waste any time considering how you would use certain things if you had them; consider, simply, how to use what you have. It is also certain that you will progress more rapidly if you make the most perfect use of what you have. In fact, the degree of rapidity with which you attain what you want will depend upon the perfection with which you use what you have. Many people are at a standstill, or find things coming their way very slowly because they are making only partial use of present means, power, and opportunities.

You may see this point more plainly by considering an analogy in nature. In the process of evolution, the squirrels developed their leaping power to its fullest extent; then a continuous effort to advance brought forth the flying squirrel, which has a membrane uniting the legs in such a way as to form a parachute and enable the animal to sail some distance beyond an ordinary leap. A little extension of the parachute jump of the flying squirrel produced the bat, which as membranous wings and can fly; and continuous flight produced the bird with feathered wings. The transition from one plane to another was accomplished simply by perfecting and extending functions. If the squirrels had not kept leaping further and further, there would have been no flying squirrel, and no power of flight. Making constructive use of the leaping power produced flight. If you are only jumping half as far as you can, you will never fly. In nature, we see that life advances from one plane to another by perfecting function on the lower plane. Whenever an organism contains more life than it can express by functioning perfectly on its own plane, it begins to perform the functions of the next higher, or larger plane. The first squirrel which began to develop the parachute membrane must have been a very perfect leaper. This is the fundamental principle of evolution, and of all attainment.

In accordance with this principle, then, you can advance only by more than filling your present place. You must do, perfectly, all that you can do now; and it is the law that by doing perfectly all that you can do now you will become able to do later things which you cannot do now. The doing to perfection of one thing invariably provides us with the equipment for doing the next larger thing, because it is a principle inherent in nature that life continuously advances. Every person who does one thing perfect is instantly presented with an opportunity to begin doing the next larger thing. This is the universal law of all life, and is unfailing. First, do perfectly all that you can do now; keep on doing it perfectly until the doing of it becomes so easy that you have surplus power left after doing it; then by this surplus power you will get a hold on the work of a higher plane, and begin to extend your correspondence with environment.

Get into a business which will use your strongest faculties, even if you must commence at the bottom; then develop those faculties to the utmost. Cultivate power-consciousness, so that you can apply your faculties successfully, and apply them in doing perfectly everything you can do now, where you are now.

Do not wait for a change of environment; it may never come. Your only way of reaching a better environment is by making constructive use of your present environment. Only the most complete use of your present environment will place you in a more desirable one.

If you wish to extend your present business, remember that you can only do it by doing in the most perfect manner the business you already have. When you put life enough into your business to more than fill it, the surplus will get you more business. Do not reach out after more until you have life to spare after doing perfectly all that you have to do now. It is of no advantage to have more work or more business than you have life to do perfectly; if that is the case, increase your vital power first. And remember, it is the perfection with which you do what you have to do now that extends your field and brings you in touch with a larger environment.

Bear in mind that the motive force which gets you what you want is life; and that what you want, in the last analysis, is only an opportunity to live more; and that, therefore, you can get what you want only through the operation of that universal law by which all life advances continuously into fuller expression. That law is that whenever an organism has more life than can find expression by functioning perfectly on a given plane, its surplus life lifts it to the next higher plane. When you put enough of yourself into your present work to do it perfectly, your surplus power will extend your work into a larger field. It is also essential that you should have in mind what you want, so that your surplus power may be turned in the right direction.

Form a clear conception of what you seek to accomplish, but do not let what you seek to accomplish interfere with doing perfectly what you have to do now. Your concept of what you want is a guide to your energies, and an inspiration to cause you to apply them to the utmost to your present work. Live for the future now. Suppose that your desire is to have a department store, and you have only capital enough to start a peanut stand. Do not try to start a department store today, on a peanut stand capital; but start the peanut stand in the full faith and confidence that you will be able to develop it into a department store. Look upon the peanut stand merely as the beginning of the department store, and make it grow; you can.

Get more business by using constructively the business you have now; get more friends by using constructively the friends you already have; get a better position by using constructively the one you now have; get more domestic happiness by the constructive use of the love that already exists in your home.

Chapter 4
Getting the Most Out of Life

You can obtain what you want only by applying your faculties to your work and your environment; you become able to apply your faculties successfully by acquiring Power-Consciousness; and you go forward by a concentration on today's work, and by doing perfectly everything that can be done at the present time. You can get what you want in the future only by concentrating all your energies upon the constructive use of whatever you are in relation with today.

An indifferent or half-hearted use of the elements in today's environment will be fatal to tomorrow's attainment.

Do not desire for today what is beyond your ability to get today; but be sure you get today the very best that can be had. Never take less than the very best that can be had at the present time; but do not waste energy by desiring what cannot be had at the present time. If you always have the best that can be had, you will continue to have better and better things, because it is a fundamental principle in the universe that life shall continually advance into more life, and into the use of more and better things; this is the principle which causes evolution.

But if you are satisfied with less than the best that can be had, you will cease to move forward. Every transaction and relation of today, whether it be business, domestic, or social, must be made a stepping stone to what you want in the future; and to accomplish this you must put into each more than enough life to fill it. There must be surplus power in everything you do. It is this surplus power which causes advancement and gets you what you want; where there is no surplus power there is no advancement and no attainment. It is the surplus of life above and beyond the functions of present environment which causes evolution; and evolution is advancing into more life, or getting what you want. Suppose, for instance, you are in trade or a profession, and wish to increase your business; it will not do, when you sell goods or service to make the matter a merely perfunctory transaction, taking the customer's money, giving him good value, and letting him go away feeling that you had no interest in the matter beyond giving him a fair deal and profiting thereby. Unless he feels that you have a personal interest in him and his needs, and that you are honestly desirous to increase his welfare, you have made a failure and are losing ground.

When you can make every customer feel that you are really trying to advance his interests as well as your own, your business will grow. It is not necessary to give premiums, or heavier weights or better values than others give to accomplish this; it is done by putting life and interest into every transaction, however small.

If you desire to change your avocation, make your present business a stepping-stone to the one you want. As long as you are in your present business, fill it with life; the surplus will tend toward what you want.

Take a live interest in every man, woman and child you meet in either a business or social way, and sincerely desire the best for them; they will soon begin to feel that your advancement is a matter of interest to them and they will unite their thoughts for your good. This will form a battery of power in your favor and will open ways of advancement for you.

If you are an employee and desire promotion, put life into everything you do; put in more than enough life and interest to fill each piece of work. But do not be servile; never be a flunkey; and above all things avoid the intellectual prostitution which is the vice of our times in many trades and most professions. I mean by this the being a mere hired apologist for and defender of immorality, graft, dishonesty, or vice in any form. The intellectual prostitute may rise in the service, but he is a lost soul. Respect yourself; be absolutely just to all; put LIFE into every act and thought and fix Power-Conscious thought upon the fact that you are entitled to promotion; it will come as soon as you can more than fill your present place in every day. If it does not come from your present employer, it will come from another; it is the law that whosoever more than fills his present place must be advanced.

But for this law there could be no evolution, and no progress; but mark well what follows. It is not enough that you should merely put surplus life into your business relations. You will not advance far if you are a good business man or employee, but a bad husband, an unjust father, or, an untrustworthy friend. Your failure in these respects will make you incapable of using your success for the advancement of life, and so you will not come under the operation of the constructive law. Many a man who fulfills the law in business is prevented from progressing because he is unkind to his wife, or deficient in some other relation of life. To come under the operation of the evolutionary force you must more than fill EVERY present relation. A telegraph operator desired to get away from the key, and get onto a small farm; and he began to move in that direction by being "good" to his wife. He "courted" her, without any reference to his desire; and from being half indifferent she became interested and eager to help; soon they had a little piece of ground in the edge of the town, and she raised poultry and superintended a garden while he "pounded the key"; now they have a farm and he has obtained his desire. You can secure the co-operation, not only of your wife but of all the people around you by putting life and interest into all your relations with them.

Put into every relation, business, domestic or social, more than enough life to fill that relation; have faith, which is Power-Consciousness; know what you want in the future, but have today the very best that can be obtained today; never be satisfied at any time with less than the best that can be had at that time, but never waste energy in desiring what is not to be had now; use all things for the advancement of life for yourself and for all with whom you are related in any way.

Follow out these principles of action and you cannot fail to get what you want; for the universe is so constructed that all things must work together for your good.

Chapter 5
The Science of Being Successful

Wealth-culture consists in making constructive use of the people and things in your environment. First, get a clear mental picture of what you want. If your present business or profession is not the one most suitable to your talents and tastes, decide upon the one which is most suitable; and determine to get into that business or profession, and to achieve the very greatest success in it. Get a clear idea of what you want to do, and get a mental concept of the utmost success in that business or profession; and determine that you will attain to that. Give a great deal of time to forming this concept or mental picture; the more clear and definite it is, the easier will be your work. The man who is not quite sure what he wants to build will put up a wobbling and shaky structure.

Know what you want, and keep the picture of it in the background of your mind night and day; let it be like a picture on the wall of your room, always in your consciousness, night and day. And then begin to move toward it. Remember that if you have not the fully developed talent now, you can develop it as you go along; you can surely do what you want to do.

It is quite likely that at present you cannot do the thing you want to do because you are not in the right environment, and have not the necessary capital; but this does not hinder you from the beginning to move toward the right environment, and from beginning to acquire capital. Remember that you move forward only by doing what you can in your present environment.

Suppose that you have only capital enough to operate a newsstand, and your great desire is to own a department store; do not get the idea that there is some magical method by which you can successfully operate a department store on a newsstand capital. There is, however, a mental science method by which you can so operate a newsstand as to certainly cause it to grow into a department store.

Consider that your newsstand is one department of the store you are going to have; fix your mind on the department store, and begin to assimilate the rest of it. You will get it, if you make every act and thought constructive.

To make every act and thought constructive, every one must convey the idea of increase. Steadily hold in mind the thought of advancement for yourself; know that you are advancing toward what you want, and act and speak in this faith. Then every word and act will convey the idea of advancement and increase to others, and they will be drawn to you.

Always remember that what all people are seeking for is increase.

First, study over the facts in regard to the great abundance until you know that there is wealth for you, and that you do not have to take this wealth from any one else. Avoid the competitive spirit. You can readily see that if there is limitless abundance there is enough for you, without robbing anyone else. Then, knowing that it is the purpose of nature that you should have what you want, reflect upon the fact that you can get it only by acting. Consider that you can act only upon your present environment; and do not try to act now upon environment of the future.

Then remember that in acting upon your present environment, you must make every act a success in itself; and that in doing this you must hold the purpose to get what you want. You can hold this purpose only as you get a clear mental picture of what you want; be sure that you have that. Also, remember that your actions will not have dynamic moving power unless you have an unwavering faith that you get what you want.

Form a clear mental picture of what you want; hold the purpose to get it; do everything perfectly, not in a servile spirit, but because you are a master mind; keep unwavering faith in your ultimate attainment of your goal, and you cannot fail to move forward.

For *Thinking Into Results* Consulting & Personal Development:
didiking.think@gmail.com
www.kingquantumthought.com

Titles in the King Quantum Thought Series:
The Science of Getting Rich, Wallace D. Wattles
The Science of Getting Rich Study Guide,
Wallace D. Wattles & Jeffrey L. King
The Science of Being Well, Wallace D. Wattles
The Science of Being Great, Wallace D. Wattles
How to Get What You Want: The Science of Being Successful,
Wallace D. Wattles
Start Getting It Done Now: Achieving Stellar Results by Better Managing Your Time, Your Projects, and Your Life, Jeffrey L. King
As a Man Thinketh, James Allen
The Hidden Power, Thomas Troward
The Edinburgh Lectures on Mental Science, Thomas Troward
The Power of Awareness, Neville Goddard

More titles being added regularly; find the current list at
www.kingquantumthought.com/resources
with links to purchase them from amazon.com.

To contact the author:
csjkingpublishing@gmail.com

www.ingramcontent.com/pod-product-compliance
Lightning Source LLC
Chambersburg PA
CBHW071707040426
42446CB00011B/1950